The Plymouth Heritage Cookbook

The Plymouth Heritage Cookbook

Lennie Bowser

Proctor Publications, LLC
ANN ARBOR, MICHIGAN, USA

Published in the USA by
Proctor Publications
PO Box 2498, Ann Arbor, MI 48106

LCCN 97–67590

Cataloging in Publications
(Prepared by Quality Books, Inc.)
Bowser, Lennie
    The Plymouth heritage cookbook / Lennie Bowser. -- 1st ed.
    p.cm.
    Includes index.
    ISBN: 1-882792-45-9

    1. Cookery--Michigan--Plymouth. 2. Plymouth (Mich.)--History.
    I. Title

TX15.2.M53B69 1997   641.59'774'33
                       QBI97-40793

First Edition
Printed in the USA

Dedication

This book is dedicated to my children, family members, and friends who have given their loving support. Also to all the caring people who had a part in building this lovely community known as Plymouth, Michigan.

Plymouth's heritage was contributed to by the people living in the surrounding areas, such as Livonia, Canton, Nankin Township (now known as Westland), Garden City, and Northville, which seems like a sister city.

In the 1930's and early 1940's, the city buses from Detroit ended their run at Evergreen Road on Plymouth Road. From that point, you could continue your journey to Plymouth via the "Special Plymouth Bus," which ran every two hours from early morning until 11:00 p.m. daily. As you continued, Plymouth Road became Main Street. You were greeted by red brick paved roads leading to the center of town, the very heart of it. Kellogg Park is in the center, surrounded by the Penn Theater, the Box Bar and Grill, the Mayflower Hotel, the Kresge five and dime, The Plymouth Savings Bank, Willowby's Shoe Store, Kroger, and many other quaint little shops. There were many historical businesses such as the Daisy Air Rifle Plant, Burroughs Corp., and the Hillside Inn (now known as Ernesto's). These places are a great part of Plymouth's history. There are also many beautiful historical homes that have become restored residences or businesses.

The caring residents of Plymouth constantly promote cultural activities and festivals, such as the Ice Festival, which draws thousands annually. And let's not forget Cloverdale, the family-owned dairy that provided us with wonderful ice cream and a place for young people to congregate. Riverside Arena was also a very prominent link to the growth of the Plymouth community.

Since 1939, children and adults formed relationships that have been everlasting, involving several generations. There was so much love and warmth generated here and many of us are still around, living in this lovely community with our families and dear friends near. I can attest to this as I am one who, as a little girl, lived in Detroit, rode the "Special Plymouth Bus," moved to the Plymouth community, and am still here and loving it. It will always be home!

Haupt Liniment Stomach Medicine

1 pint of alcohol
1 oz. Chloroform
1 oz. tincture of opium
2 oz. tincture of opium camphorate
2 oz. tincture of Capsicum
1 oz. Sulphuric ether
4 drops oil of peppermint
1 drahm spirits camphor
1 oz. of water
color with tincture
of red saunders 2 oz.

Circa 1850 — Hand written recipe from a housewife's
notebook. Not recommended for 1997 use.
The Plymouth Historical Museum Collections

Contents

Preface

First and foremost, this is not a "low-fat" cookbook. There are many experts and professionals out there to guide us in cooking with lower fat content.

In some instances, you will find a suggestion for a substitute ingredient that works well in the recipe without changing the flavor too much. If you wish to cut fat content from any of these recipes, simply make exchanges from particular food groups, such as using half percent or low-fat evaporated milk in place of whole milk. Instead of using eggs, use Eggbeaters or other egg substitutes. When cooking meat dishes, purchase leaner cuts of meat or trim the fat before preparation. Use ground round rather than hamburger or ground chuck.

Most of these recipes are basic old-fashioned cooking. Eat the foods you like and learn to make adjustments in the preparation. Use these basics and create your own style of cooking. Everything in this cookbook has been prepared and taste-tested in the kitchen of the author. Keep it simple and enjoy the cooking and the food. . .

I apologize to those who submitted recipes or to business owners who were not included in this book. Depending on the response, however, there may be a Volume Two.

Introduction

This book is about sharing a heritage as well as a collection of recipes. It all began when I was visiting my son and his family in Huntsville, Alabama. My son and his wife are ice-skating coaches and travel often. On this occasion, I went to Huntsville and stayed with the children, Christopher and Cassandra. When I would prepare a meal or a particular dish, Christopher would say, "Grandma, this is so good. . .give my mom the recipe!"

When I returned home, I began writing recipes out to simplify the directions and proceeded to type and assemble a small book for Christopher for Christmas. My sister Marilyn was ill with cancer at this time and I spent a lot of time with her. I was always writing in my notebook and we would talk about recipes. She became very interested in my project and suggested, "Why not a family cookbook?" Her enthusiasm grew and was my inspiration to keep going with it.

I began to collect recipes from the family and found recipes from friends and neighbors. I realized there was a wonderful bond within the community here. I decided to include little stories and a history about the community where Christopher's "Michigan family" lives. (He refers to us this way.)

Having lived most of my life in Plymouth or in the surrounding areas of Livonia, Westland, and Canton, I began to recognize that Plymouth had a great deal of influence on my life. I worked at Burroughs in the 1950's, took evening classes at Plymouth High, and I was "Miss Minerva" in the July 4th pageant in 1952. Most of my clothes and shoes were purchased from Minerva's, Harvi's, Minerva-Dunning's, and Willoughby's, and furniture from Blunks, Inc. My father was born in England and when I first brought him to Plymouth, his first comment was, "I feel like I'm back in England." His funeral services were held at Schrader's in April of 1950, as were many of our family members.

Thus came *The Plymouth Heritage Cookbook*. Plymouth's heritage is about the people who developed the kind of community it is today. The name itself is a strong statement of what the people wanted to project. It began to show in the architecture of their homes, their storefronts, their manner of dress, and the festivals. It was all a reflection of their New England heritage.

There are some very good writings by Sam Hudson in our libraries and the Plymouth Historical Museum. Mr. Hudson also wrote for the *Plymouth Observer*. His accountings of Plymouth history are very detailed and were written during the 1960's and 1970's when he was able to interview some of the living descendants of the original settlers. For an in-depth study or some very good reading, I recommend them. It helps understand the attraction to this community.

My description of Plymouth's heritage highlights the people and important events from its past. I also include "history in the making" with photographs of today's Plymouth. There are many changes occurring in this lovely community as we approach the year 2000.

The Early Days of Plymouth

The story of Plymouth, Michigan almost reads like a good recipe. When you assemble the right ingredients, using the best quality ingredients available, your efforts can hardly fail. And so it is with the building of a community such as this. The hearts of the people are visible in the structure and beauty of their city, and the strength and determination of their heritage is treasured and protected. My tribute to this lovely city is to share this collection of recipes along with some of its early history, and some of the "history in the making." For those who don't use our libraries or visit our museums, perhaps your interest can be stimulated as you prepare your meals.

To begin, in 1820, Congress passed a Land Act which allowed the sale of public land in this territory of Michigan. Lewis Cass was Governor and had secured by treaty with the Indians all of the land south of Grand River. This removed most of the "hostile" Indians. The Potawatomi were the tribe known to this area, though they were not directly in the area to be known as Plymouth.

In 1824, settlers began to arrive from New England and New York, including Allen and William Tibbits who settled on 800 acres.

In 1825, the Erie Canal opened between New York and Buffalo, opening the doors to the Great Lakes region. Hardy people such as William Starkweather appeared. He built the first temporary structure where the Mayflower Hotel stands today. His wife Keziah Benjamin Starkweather was the first white woman to live in Plymouth. They had brought one son, Albert, from New York when they migrated here. George Anson Starkweather was the second son born here and was grandfather to Karl "Hillmer" Starkweather. Karl was born to George's daughter and her husband so his last name was Hillmer. He was so proud of the Starkweather heritage, he had his last name legally changed to Starkweather in Probate Court. His love for his grandfather prompted him to leave his job at Daisy Air Rifle years later to care for his ailing grandfather prior to his death.

William Starkweather purchased a 240 acre parcel which encompassed all of what is now downtown Plymouth and much of the residential area surrounding it. He began selling off small parcels and quadrupled his original investment. He then purchased another 80 acres north of his original holdings. John Kellogg arrived in 1832 and acquired 212 acres of this downtown acreage. Therefore, at different times, these two men owned all of what is now downtown Plymouth. George Anson Starkweather became a prominent civic leader in both the Township and the Village. He was a self made man who believed in hard work and family values. He has been memorialized in the name of the Starkweather school and a street that bears his name.

Also in 1825, Abraham B. Markham arrived in December at the age of 28. Markham's accounting in history is one of backpacking all the way from East Bloomfield, New York via Buffalo and Canada. He purchased 80 acres in Plymouth Township. He talks of cabin raisings and hard work but no unhappiness. Everyone was kind and generous. He was a very hardy pioneer who could clear an acre in a week, logs chopped and fit for logging. Markham also held many offices in the early days. He was fence viewer, road master, collector, constable, and secretary of the meeting in February 1827 when the town was named, and was elected Township Clerk at the first meeting. The first tax levied was $154.50 and Markham was the collector. There were 140 taxpayers.

In 1827, the name "Plymouth" was proposed by William Bartow, a member of the Territorial Legislative Council. He declared that the name was "historic and patriotic" as well as suitable because many of the settlers had lived near Plymouth Rock in Massachusetts. Governor Cass approved  the name in April 1827. The Township included Canton and Northville, which would become separate townships – Canton in 1834 and Northville in 1898.

In 1832, John Kellogg arrived from New York. By 1835, he had acquired most of the downtown property, which had been sold off to several other settlers by George A. Starkweather. It was said that when he arrived with his family, he had a chest full of gold coins from the sale of a hotel and warehouse in New York. Kellogg was 46 when he arrived here and lived to

be 85. He opened the Plymouth Hotel, a potash and soap factory, and sold off business and residential lots all around what now is Kellogg Park. The park had been called the Village Green at one time and, prior to 1867, the City acquired the park, although there is no record as to how. It was always the center of activity for gatherings and it was said that it might have been by common consent. The fact that Kellogg or his heirs never protested leaves no doubt that Plymouth owes much gratitude to this family.

The name "Plymouth" was a strong statement of the kind of community the people wanted to project. A reflection of their New England heritage began to show in the architecture of the homes, the storefronts, and the way they dressed. For such a small community when compared to cities the size of Detroit, for instance, the number of outstanding citizens who became wealthy or made notable contributions to not only the city of Plymouth, but also to their country, is remarkable. A few of these people are particularly noteworthy.

1829 – 1900: Theodatus Timothy Lyon was a self taught authority in the science and practice of growing fruit, known as a pomologist or horticulturist. He developed the basic fruit variety list for the U.S. Dept. of Agriculture through his work in horticulture. He was also a pioneer in railroad construction and, in the 1860's, became president of two railroad lines that would become the Pere Marquette Railway System.

1840 – 1890: Ebeneezer Jenckes Penniman was 36 when he arrived here in 1840. He purchased land from John Kellogg and opened a country store. He was Township Supervisor from 1842 to 1844 and in 1850. He was a land developer, merchant, banker, and politician, and served in the U.S. Congress from 1851 to 1853. He was among  those who founded the Republican party "under the oaks" at Jackson, Michigan. He was named president of the First National Bank of Plymouth in 1871. He was Plymouth's wealthiest resident at this time. E.J. Penniman died in 1890 and was buried in Riverside Cemetery. Twenty years later, Sutton Street was renamed Penniman Avenue on petition of Mrs. S.M. Reed and others in his honor.

In 1840, the population in Plymouth was 2,163 and the population in Detroit was 9,102. Today in 1997, Plymouth City has a population of 9,560 residents. Plymouth Township has 24,600. In 1867, Plymouth was incorporated as a Village with 129 votes coming from the men of the village as women did not have the vote yet.

Main Street burned down twice. The building section between Penniman Avenue and Ann Arbor Trail facing Kellogg Park was lost. Fires occurred both in 1856 and in 1893.

According to Nettie Dibble's historical writings from the 1930's, the only industries in Plymouth in the early years were the grist and saw mills. There were seven grist mills and six saw mills in the Township of Plymouth, all doing a thriving business. One of these mills was a grist mill purchased by David Wilcox in 1879 and who, with his sons George H. and John Charles, owned it for 40 years. A descendant of David Wilcox, Johnston H. (Jack) Wilcox, is still living in the impressive Wilcox House at the corner of Union Street and Ann Arbor Trail. It was built by William  (Phil) Markham in 1903 for his secretary whom he married after the death of his wife. His affair at the turn of the century so shocked the town that they never accepted the couple. The Wilcox family purchased the home from Markham in 1911.

I was invited to visit with Jack Wilcox at the Wilcox House in June of 1997. We sat on the porch of his wonderful old home and Jack spoke freely about his beloved Plymouth and some of his concerns. He hopes that one day, the two Plymouths, the city and the township, will merge, eliminating the duplication of services. I realized as he reminisced that Jack has a stong sense of responsibility as a historian and as a citizen. He has served in the Historical Society, the Chamber of Commerce, and various planning commissions and is very often invited to speak at Kiwanis and Rotary meetings. He travels often to England and China and is well versed in Chinese traditions and economic development. Jack Wilcox was 80 years of age on June 12, 1997, and has certainly given much of his life to the betterment and heritage of Plymouth.

Plymouth was a stage coach stop on the route from Detroit to Ann Arbor. This created a need for hotels and restaurants. The first hotel was the Plymouth Hotel, established by John Kellogg at the corner of Main Street and Ann Arbor Trail. Another was Peter Fralick's Union Hall. In 1857, after the first fire, the Adams House emerged and was managed by Thomas Whipple. It was the site of the  first election in 1867. In 1868, the Bode House was established by the Bode family on Main Street near the railroad tracks and is still operating today as a restaurant. In the 1890's, another Plymouth Hotel emerged in the same location as the first. This was operated by J.G. Streng in 1898. The last owner was Ralph J. Lorenz who had it razed in 1927 as it was condemned.

Another hotel in the early 1900's was the Hotel Anderine, formerly the Hotel Victor, operated by George Streng, a cousin of Jacob Streng who also ran a restaurant. Jacob Streng was father to Mrs. Margaret Stremich who was well known in the community for her many years at the Hillside Inn. Margaret Streng had been raised in the restaurant business and she and her husband opened a restaurant in the  old Streng homestead, which they originally named Hillside Barbecue. Her husband died in 1948 and she managed alone until 1951 when she took her nephew, Robert Stremich, as partner. Mrs. Stremich retired in 1970. The Hillside Inn opened in 1934 with seating capacity of 48. In 1974, the seating capacity was 430. The Hillside Inn changed hands and is now called Ernesto's. The new owner is Salvatore "Sam" Messina. It is even more beautiful with outdoor seating overlooking the park drive and woods, and the balcony is screened in for protection from insects. It is one of the finest dining places around the area.

Plymouth had a brewery operated by Fred Dohmstreich on his farm from about 1860 to 1862. The place then became Wildey's Cheese Factory and operated until 1876.

In the 1890's, there were two cigar manufacturing companies – The Plymouth Cigar Company and a one-man operation by George Springer who had a shop in his home. His brand names included Our Senator, The Plymouth Mail, Springer's Best, Chief Hunter, Horseman's Favorite, Hotel Plymouth, Hotel Victor, and Plymouth Belle. Springer gave up the cigar business for law enforcement as Deputy Sheriff of Plymouth Township in 1900 and Village Marshall in 1912. He remained in office until 1932. It was said that he was no one to mess with.

In 1885, the air rifle era would begin with the manufacture of a toy rifle called the "Chicago" at the Markham Manufacturing Company. The plant was located in the building that now houses The Plymouth Landing restaurant. A second air rifle plant would emerge out of the Plymouth Windmill Company on Union Street. It would be named The Daisy Air Rifle Company in 1895. Charlie Bennett traveled the world selling the air rifle and made Plymouth the air rifle center of the world. The company was Plymouth's largest employer.

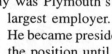

Markham Building

He became president of Daisy and held the position until his death in 1956 at the age of 94. Lewis Cass Hough, a Michigan Senator, was one of the founders of Daisy and his son, Edward C. Hough, was general manager and became president when Bennett died. Cass Hough made the startling announcement in November 1957 that Daisy would move the entire operation to Rogers, Arkansas. This ended the 75 year connection with Plymouth. Governor Williams' economic policies were given as the reason for the move.

Phil Markham decided to leave Plymouth in 1911. As mentioned earlier, the town had refused to accept the second Mrs. Markham, so he left E.S. Roe to run his air rifle plant and moved to Hollywood. He sold the large, white house to George Wilcox of the Wilcox Mill Family. Eventually, the company was bought out by Daisy. E.C. Hough and C.H. Bennett personally bought 90% of the stock and in 1931, after Markham died, Daisy bought the rest. Markham had bought property in the country in California which became Hollywood Boulevard and Vine Street. At the time of his death, he owned approximately 100 parcels of land in and around Los Angeles and all were leased for 99 years.

In the 1890's, Henry Ford visited Plymouth at the request of Lafayette Dean. Ford was hired from Dearborn as a well-known young mechanic to set up some machinery. His next visit was in 1903. He was looking for investors for his new business, The Ford Motor Company. He offered Charlie Bennett, the president of Daisy, one half of his new company for a $50,000 investment. Bennett did not personally have enough money and Daisy wouldn't commit, so negotiations ended as did Plymouth's opportunity to be home of Ford Motor Company. However, Ford did open a village plant in place of the Wilcox Flour Mill at Wilcox pond in 1923. The late Karl Starkweather was employed there from 1922 to 1947. The plant closed then, the year Henry Ford died. Karl then transferred to the Waterford plant until retiring in 1955.

From 1914 to 1916, the Alter Motor car was built in Plymouth. Big things were expected as the car was well received by the buying public. It was thought that Plymouth could become the Motor City of the Midwest. It was reported in the Plymouth Mail in 1916 to have "that classy look and finish of higher priced cars." The price was $685. However, the car was not a selling success and the company was dissolved in January 1917. The Plymouth Historical Museum on Main Street has the only known Alter vehicle on display in the United States.

 In 1871, the railroads came to Plymouth. George Anson Starkweather believed the depot area in the North Village would be the new center of activity and built a new store building at the corner of Starkweather and Liberty. In 1875, he built the family home located diagonally from the store. The home is an historic landmark. This part of Plymouth is now referred to as the "Old Village."

By 1916, Plymouth was a busy railroad center and more than one hundred residents were on the Pere Marquette's payroll. There were 18 passenger trains daily in and out of Plymouth over a twenty-four hour period plus freight trains. Although there were economic advantages that came with railroads, it is also inconvenient to have eight crossings in a town two and a half miles square. The noise and smoke were bad, also.

A major train wreck in U.S. history was at Van Sickle Cut, about four miles east of

Main and Penniman Streets

Plymouth, on July 20, 1907. It was referred to as "the Salem Wreck." A special excursion train with ten passenger cars and a baggage car loaded with 800 people, including the crew, collided head-on with a six car freight train. The families on the excursion train were enroute from Ionia to Detroit where they were to take a chartered boat to Belle Isle for an annual picnic. Thirty-three died and 100 were injured. The railroad is now owned by C & O.

Wooden sidewalks were built in Plymouth in 1872. The roads were one-way wooden plank roads that ran from Detroit to Northville. Wagons were driven on the planks when they were loaded and were driven on the dirt when unloaded for the return trip. There were toll gates set up at different areas where users paid for using the wooden roads. The Plymouth toll gate was located at the corner of North Main and Mill Street. Plymouth Plank Road, as it was then called, ran all the way to Grand River, where it joined a two plank road into Detroit. These roads were owned and operated by private corporations.

In 1891, L.C. Hough & Sons of the Plymouth Elevator Company bought some of the first cement brought into the U.S. from Germany. L.C. Hough, W.O. Allen, T.C. Sherwood, and E.C. Leach all lived along North Main Street and installed the first concrete sidewalks that lasted more than fifty years.

In 1908, Fred Bennett, then Village president, led the drive against all opposition to brick pave Main Street. According to Sam Hudson's accounting from Karl Starkweather, the entire job was done by one man. He used 550,000 bricks and crowds would gather to watch him work. The job was completed in November 1908. The brick road lasted for more than a century and is still there giving a sturdy base to the present road.

In 1932, Plymouth Village became a city, with a city manager and commission. Many times through the years, Plymouth City has attempted to annex Plymouth Township, or parts of it. The Township has always voted it down. However, perhaps the city's charm and good management can be attributed to having solid control of their small community. Also, many good things are accomplished with cooperation from the surrounding townships. There are no boundaries when you see the support from these communities during the festivals held in the city. The festivals are sponsored by the many local organizations which are the backbone and strength of the community. The Fall Festival grew from a community family picnic sponsored by the Plymouth Rotary Club and is the greatest evidence of what community cooperation can do.

Mayflower Hotel

The Mayflower Hotel was opened in November 1927 at a cost of $209,000. The ground-breaking was on April 25, 1927. On November 10, 1927, a dedication banquet was held in the new crystal dining room of the hotel, attended by 200 stockholders and other citizens. Local residents had assembled and raised the funds by selling stock. The money was raised in only six hours.

Ralph G. Lorenz acquired the hotel in 1965 after being manger from 1939 to 1965. The Mayflower continued to operate under the Lorenz family until 1996. The new owners, Matt and Neran Karmo, are now undergoing total renovation and reconstruction in 1997. They have a projected completion date for late 1997 or possibly Spring of 1998. It will boast new dining rooms, a cafe and lounge, a new lobby, banquet facilities for 200 guests, and gift displays. All access will be from the inside of the building with easy accessibility to all facilities. There will be a five-star chef serving the finest cuisine at moderate prices. There will also be entertainment on a lower level.

Riverside Arena

The Riverside Arena was also a very prominent link to Plymouth from May 30, 1940 when it first opened to this very day. In fact, until 1950 with the birth of Livonia, the arena's mailing address was 36635 Plymouth Road, Plymouth, Michigan. The link connected young people to social and competitive adventures and got many parents involved in skating rink club activities. You can hardly talk to a resident in Plymouth, Canton, Northville, Livonia, Westland, Wayne or Garden City that didn't skate at Riverside. Many became artistic and competitive achievers and are now national and international skating champions. Parents became officers in the Figure and Dance Club and took care of the financial and promotional activities of the skating club.

Left: author Lennie Bowser and daughter, 1952. Center: Lionel LaMay, owner of Riverside Arena, 1946. Top right: Jim Bowser & Nancy Burghoff, Professional World Champions Ice Dancing, Spain, 1983. Bottom right: Jean O'Mara & George Petro, National Paris Champions, 1944.

Lionel "Ona" LaMay and his wife, Lee, operated the roller rink and brother Clayton LaMay taught skating for many years. Ona told me a long time ago that he had retired from owning a C.F. Smith grocery store in Grandale and was leaving town with his family packed in the car, when he had a flat tire at the site where he built the rink. He said he looked around, thought the area was beautiful, and decided that God was giving him a message to stay and do something here. He began with a tent and a portable skating surface and eventually built one of the most elaborate roller skating rinks in Michigan.

The rink is still well-managed by their children, Lionel, Leo, and Analee. In 1990, they celebrated their 50th anniversary with a large reunion. The Mayor of Livonia attended as did other city officials for an award ceremony honoring the family's contribution to the community. There was food, wine, dancing to a live orchestra, and later, open skating. There were past skaters from three generations there and a wonderful reunion was had by all. The family is planning another reunion for their 60th anniversary in May of 2000.

Plymouth Community Arts Council

The council was founded by Joanne Winkleman Hulce to promote community visual art, music, dance, and drama. They also sponsor classes, children's theater, craft shows, and music in Kellogg Park. Seniors are urged to participate in the classes  and to get involved and lend support to this very worthy cause. Mrs. Hulce is a very energetic lady and is the heartbeat of this organization. Her son, Tom Hulce, is an achiever from Plymouth who became an actor and starred in the movie Amadeus in 1984. The Arts Council is now located in a beautiful new location on Sheldon Road in Plymouth.

Plymouth Historical Museum

In June 1948, the Plymouth Historical Society was formed. Its purpose  was to establish a historical museum in Plymouth to house and preserve historical material from Plymouth and surrounding communities. The present location on Main Street was acquired through the generosity of Margaret Dunning, a long-time resident and businesswoman in the city, and was donated in memory of her parents Charles A. and Bessie I. Dunning, the Society's first curator. The Plymouth Historical Society is dedicated to preserving the heritage of Plymouth and surrounding communities. Scholars and researchers are encouraged to use the Archives for local and regional history. Microfilming and a reader-printer is available for reasearchers and computers have been installed. Exhibits include Victorian rooms, decorated in the style of the late 1800's, and Main Street shops as they appeared in the early days of Plymouth. There is also a gift shop with unusual and historic gift items as well as a Daisy Air Rifle display and a 1915 model of the Alter Car. There are old books, pictures, legal documents, journals, and genealogies that have been preserved on microfilm.

Radio Station WSDP

The Plymouth/Canton public school district is one of the finest in Michigan. The high school students have their own radio station. Station WSDP 88.1 FM is located in the Salem High School at Joy Road and Canton

Center. Plymouth/Canton High and Salem High School both participate in the program. The station first aired February 14, 1972, and is on air 15 hours per day, Monday through Friday from 8 AM to 11 PM. They play music, do local news at 5:30 with a "national feature," weather, and sports. The operation is staffed by 30 to 40 students. It is an extracurricular activity, though some credits are earned. There is an application process and auditions in the fall and spring for students who are interested.
Interview: Bill Keith and Niraj Patel

Plymouth Community Band

There are free performances during the summer at Kellogg Park and at other times at the Canton Little Theater. They do 15 to 20 concerts annually. The band is a very important part of the community and has always shared in important events of the city. In the early days of Plymouth, the band was always shown in pictures taken of the town festivals. One of them was displayed in Henry Ford's office.

Plymouth Theater Guild

The guild performs comedies, dramas, musicals, and mysteries four times per year at the Water Tower Theater in Northville. Plymouth residents have shown a great deal of interest in theatrical arts dating back to the early 1900's. "Word of Honor", a film starring Karl Malden, was filmed in Plymouth in 1980.

Plymouth Symphony Orchestra

They Symphony performs ten concerts per year at various locations with tickets costing from $8.00 to $45.00. The Plymouth Symphony League was established in 1954 to assist the Symphony Society in raising funds to support the Symphony Orchestra. This is a well respected group throughout the state under the leadership of Russell Reed, Conductor.

Box Bar and Grill

"The puritanical nonsense of excluding children – and therefore to some extent women – from pubs has turned these places into mere boozing shops instead of the family gathering places they

ought to be." –George Orwell

The historical Box Bar and Grill is renowned for its great sandwiches, and for beer lovers, they carry brands from 22 countries. A total of 228 bottled brands and 7 draft beers on tap. The above quote appears on their menu.

Lower Town Grill

Located at 195 W. Liberty at the corner of Starkweather in the historical building built by George Starkweather in the early 1870's. The restaurant is now operated by Steve Williams who has maintained the atmosphere of an era from the early days of Plymouth mixed with today's food and music. This part of town is call the Old Village, often referred to as Lower Town. There are many historical buildings in this village that are now small businesses that add great charm to the city.

Cozy Cafe

The original Cozy Cafe opened in Plymouth in September of 1978. Tina and Nick Ristich became the new owners of Cozy and opened on February 13, 1982. Tina has a warmth and sincerity that reaches out and makes you feel glad you came in. This warmth and charm is also evident in the decor and the staff as they serve and make you feel welcome. Manager Susan carefully oversees the operation and reflects the same gracious warmth. The dining area has been expanded inside and there is also sidewalk cafe dining on the outside. Cozy is famous for their crepes, crustless quiches, and wonderful pies, cakes, and cinnamon rolls baked fresh every-

day in their upstairs bakery. They serve breakfast, lunch, and dinner and have daily specials. The menu also includes flavored coffees and herbal teas. Cozy has been honored by being included in the Cats Meow Collection, small wooden, handpainted replicas of many historical buildings and store fronts in Plymouth, which will be available for sale in the restuarant. The Ristich family also owns and operates Plymouth Manor Catering on Main Street, which caters parties up to 400 guests.

Cafe Bon Homme

This wonderful, upscale restaurant serves delicious food within a beautiful setting. Owned by Greg and Susan Goodman, it is located at 844 Penniman.

Daly's Drive In

One of the last of the "cruising" places for young folks. Still serving "at the curb" the favorite hot dogs, hamburgers, and milkshakes. Park, order, and eat in your car or be served inside.

Station 885

Built on the site of the old freight house on Starkweather next to the railroad tracks, this restaurant has a unique atmosphere with a toy train roaming throughout the lounge and dining rooms just below ceiling level. The whole family is involved in the operation, including an artist who painted a wonderful mural in the lobby which exhibits a whole wall of an historic look at Plymouth. A wide variety menu including pizza for your dining experience. There is also combo entertainment on certain nights in the cocktail lounge, a spiral staircase to the second level which is more intimate, and a screened-in patio for outdoor dining. Owners: Jerry and Joyce Costanza.

Wild Wings Gallery

Another Plymouth treasure at 338 South Main Street at the corner of Ann Arbor Trail. It is a gallery of paintings, prints, and home furnishings appealing to the sportsman to add a rustic touch to your home decor. A very friendly family operation, owned by Kal Jahara.

Gabriala's

A unique shop located at 322 S. Main Street facing Kellogg Park. Gabriala's has been in Plymouth since 1983 and is well known for a vast variety of gift selections, paintings, prints, and is the largest distriubtor of the Cat's Meow Collection in the U.S. It will be expanding in 1997 by another 1,000 sq. feet in the lower level. The new level will be known as Gabriala's Hidden Secrets and will feature a Nite Lite and Lighting Gallery as well as home furnishings such as accent tables, unique mirrors, an office display, and a dining display. Willoughby's was previously at this site. Owner: Larry Bird

Within its 173-year history, the community of Plymouth has grown and flourished, and has cultivated many successful citizens. However, throughout all of its changes, this small village has never lost its heart. It has been a privilege to incorporate some of this history into my cookbook and, during my research, I learned much about what makes a community what it is. It is the strength of our heritage that makes us prosper and thrive. "And oh what a heritage Plymouth has!"

Sources
Community Crier, March 1990. 1993 Talk of the Town.
Gilbert, Helen Francis. *Tonquish Tales, Volume 2*, 1984.
Hudson, Sam. *The Story of Plymouth Michigan: A Midwest Microcosm*, 1976; *Pictures of Plymouth: Past and Present*, 1968.
Plymouth Historical Museum. Old recipes and pictures, 1837 – 1900's.
Plymouth Observer, Great Moments in Plymouth History.
Ann Arbor News, Mayflower Hotel: Plymouth's Rock, 1990.

1997 Interviews:
Betty Buzuvis, Owner of The Paper Parade
Joann Hulce, Founder of Plymouth Community Arts Council
Matt and Neron Karmo, Owners of Mayflower Hotel
Lionel LaMay, Owner of Riverside Arena
Steve Mansfield, Owner of Heide's Flowers & Gifts
Jim Plakas, Owner of The Plymouth Landing
Tina Ristich, Owner of The Cozy Cafe
Jack Wilcox
Steve Williams, Owner of Lower Town Grill

Equip Your Kitchen

You will be more efficient and time in the kitchen will be more pleasant if you have the right equipment. The following list will be your guide to a good start. Invest in good heavy-duty pans and utensils. They can last a lifetime and heavy pans make the difference, especially when cooking meat. I recommend buying your equipment at commercial restaurant stores, such as Gordon Foods, a gourmet kitchen store or a good department store, such as Hudson's or J.C. Penney's.

Six-quart dutch oven
Six- or eight-quart stock pot
8- or 10-inch small heavy-duty wok (stovetop type)
3 good frying pans of different sizes with lids
Large electric frying pan
Large spatter screen
1-quart, 2-quart, and 3-quart sauce pans
Small and large oval roaster
5- or 6-quart crock pot
2 large cookie sheets and cookie cutters
Cake and pie pans
Loaf pans for bread
Measuring cups and spoons with clear markings
Stainless steel mixing bowls
Mixer or food processor
Potato masher
Various utensils: wooden spoons, spatulas and scrapers, potato peeler, tongs, stainless steel slotted spoons, heavy-duty forks, ladles, pastry brushes, baster, funnel, biscuit and doughnut cutter
Set of good kitchen knives, steak knives, paring and slicing knives
Chopping boards
Strainers of different sizes
Rolling pin
Steamer, automatic or insert for pan
Hot pads and trivets
Food thermometer
Storage containers

Glossary of Terms

Au gratin: a baked dish with cheese added

Au jus: natural meat juices

Bake: to cook in the oven, covered or uncovered

Baste: to pour juices over food during cooking with spoon, ladle or baster

Blake: lightly break apart with fork

Blanche: to precook in boiling water for a short time

Boil: to cook in hot, boiling water for a short time

Braise: to cook slowly, covered, in own juice or a little liquid

Broil: to cook using direct heat or coals

Brown: to cook quickly on high heat, each side, before reducing heat

Breading: to coat with bread or cracker crumbs

Chop or dice: cut in pieces

Fillet: meat or fish without bones

Fold: to gently mix ingredients by cutting through to bottom and bringing batter up and over until blended

Fry: to cook in a small amount of oil (pan fry) or in a large amount of oil (deep fry)

Knead: to work dough by folding and pressing with hand or rolling pin

Marinate: to soak food in liquid to flavor and tenderize

Mince: to chop very fine

Parboil: to boil before further cooking, removing fat and softening

Poach: to cook in hot, boiling water, gently basting

Precook: to partially cook to finish at a later time

Saute: to brown or cook in butter, gently, in a frying pan

Scallop: to bake in casserole with sauce or liquid

Sear: to lightly cook on each side with hot oil

Conversions

Table of Measurements:

3 tsp. = 1 Tbs.

4 Tbs. = 1/4 cup

8 Tbs. = 1/2 cup

16 Tbs. = 1 cup

1 oz. = 28.35 gms.

1 gram = 0.035 oz.

1 cup = 8 oz.

1 cup = 1/2 pint

2 cups = 1 pint

4 cups = 1 quart

4 quarts = 1 gallon

1 liter = 1.06 quarts

Oven Chart:

Very slow oven	250° – 275°	Slow oven	300° – 325°
Moderate oven	350° – 375°	Hot oven	400° – 425°
Very hot oven	450° – 475°	Extremely hot oven	500° – 525°

Broiling:

Steaks: 1 inch thick, 3 – 5 inches from heat

	Rare	8 – 10 minutes
	Medium	12 – 14
	Well done	18 – 20

2 inches thick, 3 – 5 inches from heat

	Rare	14 – 20 minutes
	Medium	30 – 35
	Well done	40 – 45

Ground round, 3/4 inch 10 minutes

Fish fillets 10 – 15 minutes

Substitutions:

1 cake compressed yeast = 1 pkg. active dry yeast

1 cup whole milk = 1/2 cup evaporated milk + 1/2 cup water

1 clove garlic = 1/8 tsp. garlic powder

1 small onion = 1 Tbs. instant minced onion

1 tsp. dry mustard = 1 Tbs. prepared mustard

1 Tbs. cornstarch = 2 Tbs. flour or 4 tsp. tapioca (for thickening)

1 cup catsup or chili sauce = 1 cup tomato sauce + 1/2 cup sugar and 2 Tbs.
    vinegar, in cooked mixtures only

Appetizers,
Dips,
&
Dressings

We may live without poetry, music and art,
We may live without conscience and live without heart,
We may live without friend, we may live without books,
But civilized man cannot live without cooks.

Helen Louise Johnson
The Enterprising Housekeeper
Published in 1906

Baked Stuffed Shrimp
Walt Zorn

16 jumbo shrimp, shelled, butterflied, and deveined
Dressing:

1 stick melted butter or margarine   **1 tsp. garlic powder**
1 cup crushed Ritz crackers   **1 Tbs. wine (optional)**

   Place shrimp in greased pan or baking dish. In sauce pan, melt butter and add garlic powder, cracker crumbs, and wine. Pile on top of shrimp. Bake at 350° for 20 minutes. May be prepared ahead and kept refrigerated until time to bake. Serves four.

Crabmeat Dip
Billie Knaggs

8 oz. cream cheese, softened   **Can of crab meat or imitation**
2 Tbs. green onion, chopped   **crab legs**
1 Tbs. lemon juice   **Pecans, finely crushed**
1/2 tsp. tabasco sauce or garlic juice **Paprika**

   Mix first four ingredients well. Add crab meat or imitation crab legs. Bake at 350° for 30 minutes. Top with pecans. Sprinkle with paprika.

Braunschweiger Pate

2 pkg. 8 oz. rolls, Oscar Mayer   **1 small onion, finely chopped**
   Braunschweiger   **2 Tbs. Hellman's mayonnaise**
8 oz. cream cheese

   Put all ingredients into mixing bowl and mix at low speed until well mixed. Chill at least one hour. Form into a mound and place on a serving plate, surrounded with assorted crackers (Ritz would be my choice). Place a pate knife in center of mound for spreading. Garnish with parsley.

Tangy Pineapple Cheese Mound
Kathie Wilde

1/2 cup apple jelly   **2 Tbs. horseradish**
1/2 cup pineapple jelly   **1 Tbs. horseradish sauce**
1 small can crushed pineapple,   **2 large packages cream cheese**
   well-drained

   In food processor or blender, mix all ingredients except cream cheese. Spoon blended mixture over chream cheese. Serve with assorted crackers. Jelly mixture can refrigerated for one week.

Saucy Kielbasa Crock

2 pkg. Echrich beef kielbasa, sliced with the skin on
1 cup seafood cocktail sauce
  Place sliced kielbasa and cocktail sauce in crockpot. Cook on high about 45 minutes. Reduce heat to low to keep warm for buffet-type serving. Have cocktail plates and forks or picks near pot.

Saucy Cheese and Crabmeat

2 8 oz. bricks cream cheese   1 cup seafood cocktail sauce
9 oz. canned crabmeat
  Place bricks of cheese on serving plate. Pour sauce over the cheese and spread with rubber spatula. Spoon crabmeat evenly over the top. Garnish with pimento olives and parsley. Surround with assorted crackers.

Pink Salmon Roll
Estel Shomaker

1 large can pink salmon   1/2 cup chopped walnuts or pecans
1 large package cream cheese   1/4 tsp. parsley (optional)
1 Tbs. minced onion
  Drain, rinse, and remove bones and skin from salmon. Place in food processor with cream cheese and minced onion. Process just enough to blend well. Form into a roll and roll in chopped nuts and parsley. Serve on fancy plate with paté knife and assorted crackers.

Minced Bologna

1 lb. Echrich garlic bologna, chopped or ground
1/2 cup onion, chopped fine
1 or 2 Tbs. sweet or dill pickle relish
Miracle Whip by spoonfuls as desired
  Use food processor or grinder for meat preparation. Mix all ingredients well and chill for one hour. Spread on cocktail rye bread or bagels, or make tiny sandwiches. Great finger food for parties. Use minced ham for a variation.

Tuna Salad for Sandwiches
Ed Searles

1 can Albacore white chunk tuna	1 tsp. green pepper, chopped fine
1 small onion, chopped fine	1 tsp. sweet relish (optional)
1 stalk celery, chopped fine	1 or 2 Tbs. Miracle Whip

Mix well and chill at least one hour. Spread on hearty bread and add crisp, fresh iceberg lettuce.

Grilled Mozzarella and Bologna Sandwich

1 slice mozzarella cheese	French or Italian bread
1 slice Echrich garlic bologna	Butter

Place cheese and bologna between two slices of bread. Butter outside of bread. Place sandwich on preheated grill on medium heat. Brown to golden on both sides, covered with lid. Serve cut in wedges on plate with a dill pickle, chips or pretzels.

Taco Dip
Debbie Sue Hershey

8 oz. sour cream
8 oz. cream cheese, for firmness
4 stalks celery, chopped small
1 green pepper, chopped
1 red pepper, minced
2 bunches green onions, chopped
2 Roma tomatoes, chopped
1/2 head iceberg lettuce, shredded fine
2 8 oz. pkgs. sharp cheddar or Mexican blend cheese
2 large bags Dorito chips

Use a mixer or food processor to mix cream cheese with sour cream. Spread as a base on plate or tray. Layer vegetables, beginning with lettuce, then celery, green pepper, red pepper, green onions, shredded cheese, and tomatoes. Use a fancy dish or tray. Serves 12. Always a party favorite.

Dill Vegetable Dip
Ed Searles

1 cup Miracle Whip salad dressing
1 cup sour cream
1/2 tsp. dill weed
1 Tbs. minced onion
1 Tbs. celery salt
Dash of Worchester sauce
      Mix all ingredients and chill one hour. Serve with fresh, fancy cut vegetables: carrots, celery, cucumbers, broccoli, cauliflower, etc.

Tex Mex Dip

First Layer:
10 oz. can bean dip, spread on bottom of dish or pan

Second Layer:
2 medium avocados, mashed
1 Tbs. lemon juice
Salt and pepper

Mix together and spread over bean dip.

Third layer:
1/2 cup sour cream
1/4 cup mayonnaise (Hellman's)
1/2 pkg. taco seasoning

Mix together and spread over second layer.

Sprinkle the following ingredients over sour cream mixture:
1/2 bunch green onions, thinly sliced
2 tomatoes, chopped
Black olives, sliced

Sprinkle grated cheddar cheese over the top. Chill 4 hours or overnight. Served with Doritos or Tostitos. A wonderful party pleaser!

Soups, Salads, & Sauces

White Cream Sauce

2 Tbs. butter, melted
2 Tbs. flour

2 cups milk
Salt and pepper

Using a 2-quart saucepan and wooden spoon, melt butter, stir in flour, and add milk gradually, stirring constantly until thickened. For a richer sauce, add 1 beaten egg yolk. For cheese sauce, add 2 cups sharp cheddar cheese.

Beer Batter

1 cup Bisquick
1 egg
1 Tbs. vegetable oil
1/2 tsp. baking soda

1/2 cup beer to thin
1/2 cup flour, seasoned with
salt and pepper

Using a fork, mix Bisquick, beer, egg, and oil. Consistency should be a little thinner than pancake batter. Batter is enough for 8 pieces of fish. Cod fillets are best for deep frying or pan frying. Rinse fish, dry on paper towels, and coat with seasoned flour before dipping into batter.

Garlic Butter Spread

1/2 lb. butter or margarine
1/8 cup garlic powder
1/8 cup romano cheese, sprinkled on top
1/8 tsp. garlic, chopped

Melt butter in saucepan, stir in garlic powder and chopped garlic. Spread both slices of bread. Place on cookie sheet and put in oven with rack at lowest position. Bake in preheated 450° oven for 3 to 4 minutes. Should be browned on both sides. For variation, add a thinly sliced onion or parmesan cheese. Bake another minute or two.

Teriyaki Sauce

1 cup soy sauce
4 cloves garlic, crushed
3 Tbs. sugar
2 tsp. lemon juice

2 Tbs. worcestershire
2 Tbs. salad oil
Pepper to taste, no salt

Mix all ingredients in storage container. Use at room temperature and marinate steak or chicken strips 4 or 5 hours. Turn occasionally. Bake or broil in oven or on skewers over coals, turning often. Cook to desired doneness.

Dill Tartar Sauce

1 cup Hellman's mayonnaise
1 Tbs. dill pickle relish

1 Tbs. horseradish sauce
1 Tbs. onion, minced

Mix all ingredients in mini food processor and pour into storage container. Chill at least one hour or overnight before serving.

Hot Fudge Sauce

2 cups sugar
14 oz. can evaporated milk
4 (1 oz.) squares chocolate

1/2 tsp. salt
1/4 cup butter
1 tsp. vanilla

In a large cup, melt chocolate and butter in microwave. In 2-quart saucepan, combine sugar, milk, salt, and melted chocolate and butter mixture. Cook over medium heat, stirring constantly until smooth and mixture thickens. Remove from heat and stir in vanilla. Serve hot or cold over ice cream or a fruit dessert. Delicious over ice cream-filled pastry shells.

Barbecue Sauce

1 cup wine vinegar
1 cup catsup
3/4 cup chopped onion
1 Tbs. prepared mustard
1 Tbs. worcestershire sauce
1 1/2 tsp. salt

1 tsp. black pepper
1/2 cup honey
2 Tbs. brown sugar
1 clove garlic, chopped
1/2 stick butter
1/2 cup water

Use 3-quart pan. Saute chopped onions and garlic in butter, lightly. Add water and vinegar, then all other ingredients. Stir well. Simmer 20 to 30 minutes, stirring frequently. Brush or ladle onto spareribs or chicken that has been parboiled to remove most of the fat. Can be stored in refrigerator in sealed container up to 4 weeks.

Cheese and Chive Sauce (for baked potatoes)

3 Tbs. butter
1 1/2 Tbs. flour
1/4 tsp. salt
1/4 tsp. pepper

1 cup milk
2 Tbs. chopped chives
2 Tbs. grated sharp
cheddar cheese

In 1-quart saucepan, melt butter. Add flour, salt, and pepper. Add milk slowly while stirring. Add chives and cheese; cook till blended. Serve over baked potatoes, opened and split. Can be prepared ahead, set aside on a cookie sheet, and placed back in oven for 10 or 15 minutes just before serving. Enough for 4 baked potatoes.

Easy Three Bean Salad

1 can green beans	1 large red onion, sliced
1 can yellow wax beans	1 green pepper, sliced

Drain beans and combine with onions and pepper in large bowl.

Dressing:

3/4 cup salad oil	1/2 cup wine vinegar
1/2 cup sugar	1 tsp. salt and 1 tsp. pepper

Pour dressing over bean mixture and refrigerate overnight. Will keep for several days.

Macaroni Salad
Donna Perry

2 cups elbow macaroni, cooked and drained
4 stalks celery, chopped
1 green pepper, chopped
1 onion, chopped (green onions are preferred)
1 cucumber, chopped
1 small jar pimento olives, drained and chopped
1/2 to 1 cup Miracle Whip (to consistency desired)
1 Tbs. dill pickle juice
4 hard boiled eggs, chopped

Mix all ingredients in large storage bowl. Cover and chill at least 2 hours before serving. For variation, add 1 can Albacore white tuna fish or diced ham. Will keep for several days in refrigerator.

Bill Dustman's Salad

2/3 part Romain lettuce	1/3 part Iceburg lettuce
4 green onions, minced	4 fresh mushrooms, sliced thin

Dressing:

2/3 part virgin olive oil	1 tsp. garlic powder, or more
1/3 part champagne or white wine vinegar	

Wash and dry lettuce and break into small pieces in large bowl. Add onions (including green parts) and chill. When ready to serve, pour in dressing and toss. Add mushrooms on top for garnish.

German Potato Salad

8 potatoes, peeled and cooked in 1 Tbs. salted water
2 stalks celery, chopped   **4 hard boiled eggs, sliced**
1 Tbs. chopped parsley   **1 medium onion, diced**
    In large mixing bowl, mix above ingredients. Set aside. In electric fry pan, cook 8 slices bacon until crisp. Drain bacon on paper towel. Leave bacon fat in pan. In 2- to 4-cup measuring pitcher, mix the following:
1 egg, beaten   **1/4 Tbs. dry mustard**
1/2 cup sugar   **1/2 cup wine vinegar**
1/2 tsp. pepper   **1/2 cup water**
1/2 Tbs. salt
    Pour mixture into bacon fat and stir until thickened over medium heat. Pour over potatoes and eggs and add crumpled bacon. Serves 8.

Mandarin Spinach Salad —Eleanor Fawcett

1 pkg. fresh spinach, rinsed and torn
1 4 oz. can mandarin orange sections, drained (reserve liquid)
4 slices bacon, fried crisp and crumbled
1/2 cup almonds, slivered and toasted
1/2 cup fresh sliced mushrooms (optional)
1 – 2 eggs, hard cooked and chopped (optional)
    Toss all ingredients in large salad bowl and chill. Serve with
Special dressing:
Mandarin orange juice from can   **1 tsp. lemon juice**
3 Tbs. salad oil   **1/8 tsp. salt**
1 Tbs. wine vinegar   **1/4 cup water**
    Shake well and chill. Toss with chilled salad just before serving.

Bing Cherry Salad —Beatrice Kropp

2 (#2) cans pitted black cherries, drained, cut in half (reserve juice)
2 (3 oz.) pkg. black cherry Jello   **1 cup cold water**
2 cups miniature marshmallows   **1 cup cherry juice from can**
1 cup sour cream   **Blanched almonds, if desired**
2 cups hot water
    Use a large lasagne pan or one or two jello molds. Dissolve marshmallows in 1 cup of hot water in microwave in a large bowl. Set aside. Heat cherry juice with 1 cup of hot water and place in large bowl with two pkgs. of Jello. Add 1 cup of cold water and stir. Add half of Jello mixture to marshmallow and place in bottom of mold or pan. Let set. Spread part of the cherries then carefully spread the sour cream. Add a little more of the Jello mix and let set. Add rest of cherries and rest of Jello mix. Add almonds at this time, sprinkled on top. Makes a large salad for 10 or 12.

Lennie Bowser

Spaghetti Salad
Marilyn Sackett

1 lb. box thin spaghetti
1 jar McCormick's salad supreme (orange color)
1 med. red onion, chopped or sliced thin
4 or 5 tomatoes, chopped in thin wedges
1 cucumber, chopped with center seeds removed to stay crisp
1 large bottle Wishbone Italian
2 stalks celery, chopped

Cook spaghetti per box directions in boiling water with salt and 1 Tbs. oil to keep noodles from sticking together. Drain and rinse in cold water. Mix all ingredients in large salad bowl and chill. Serves 20 at the family picnic.

Note: Don't overcook pasta or it will be soggy.

Green Jello Salad
Jane Matthews Bowser

1 box of lime and 1 box of lemon Jello (3 oz.)

1 cup boiling water	**1 cup evaporated milk**
1 pint small curd cottage cheese	**1 can crushed pineapple**
1 cup Hellman's mayonnaise	**1 cup chopped walnuts**

Mix jello with water. Cool but don't let set (about 15 or 20 min. in refrigerator). Add all ingredients in a jello mold or oblong baking dish. Let set in refrigerator about 4 hours. Cut into squares and serve on a lettuce leaf. Nice served with baked ham, ham steak or baked chicken. Serves 12.

French Onion Soup

4 large onions, sliced	**2 Tbs. butter**
6 cups water	**6 beef bouillon cubes**
	or Tbs. Minors beef base

Use stock pot or dutch oven. Saute sliced onions in butter until slightly browned. Add water and beef base or bouillon. Bring to boil and simmer at least 1 hour. Can be served with croutons and grated parmesan cheese sprinkled on top. Or bake a slice of mozzarella cheese on top for 10 minutes in a hot oven. You will need soup crocks to do this or bowls that are oven safe. Good served with bread or garlic toast.

Cabbage Soup
Marilyn Sackett

46 oz. can tomato juice
46 oz. water
1 small head cabbage, shredded
1 to 2 cups celery, chopped
1 green pepper, chopped
1 large onion, chopped
4 medium tomatoes chopped or 1 can stewed tomatoes (16 oz.)
4 beef bouillon cubes
1/2 tsp. oregano
1/2 tsp. garlic powder
1/2 Tbs. parsley
Dash cayenne pepper

Simmer ingredients in large stock pot for 2 hours. Add salt and pepper.

Cabbage Soup Diet

1 head cabbage
6 onions, chopped
2 green bell peppers, minced
1 bunch scallions, chopped
6 stalks celery, chopped
6 carrots, chopped
2 cups fresh green beans or 1 16 oz. can
2 cubes beef bouillon
1 large can V-8 juice
1 28 oz. can stewed and diced tomatoes
1 pkg. Lipton Onion Soup Mix
1 to 2 Tbs. salt (to taste)
1 tsp. pepper (to taste)

In a stock pot, combine all chopped vegetables and seasonings. Add enough water to cover well. Bring to boil for 10 min. Reduce heat and simmer until vegetables are tender and full of flavor, about 2 hrs. Makes 6 quarts. Store in refrigerator. Will keep nicely for one week. Eat as much as you want, whenever you want. Per cup: approx. 34 calories, 1 gm. protein, 8 gms. carbohydrates, trace fat, 0 mg. cholesterol, trace saturated fat, 64 mg. sodium.

Potato Salad

8 or 10 potatoes
6 eggs
1 onion, diced (green onions are best)
1 green pepper, diced
1 cup celery, diced
1 cup cucumber, seeds removed
and diced
Salt and pepper
1 or 2 cups Miracle Whip (thin a little with Wishbone Italian dressing)

Cover potatoes with water in 6-quart dutch oven. Add 1 Tbs. salt. Cook potatoes 30 to 40 min. until tender. Cool, peel, and cut in small chunks. Hard boil eggs 10 minutes. Cool and peel under cold water and dice. Mix all ingredients, except dressing, in large bowl. Sprinkle salt and pepper throughout. Add dressing and mix well. Chill about 4 hours before serving.

Cabbage Soup Plus

1 small head cabbage, chopped
6 or 8 carrots, sliced
1 large onion, sliced
2 large cans stewed tomatoes
1 cup fresh, cut green beans
4 stalks celery, chopped
1 bay leaf
2 beef bouillon cubes
1 Tbs. salt or more to taste
1/2 to 1 tsp. pepper to taste

Put all prepared vegetables in dutch oven or stock pot. Cover well with water. Add stewed tomatoes, bay leaf, bouillon, and seasonings. Bring to boil. Reduce heat to med. low and simmer, covered, for 2 to 3 hours. Taste again for seasoning. Note: Keep well covered with water as this is a soup. Because of the amount of vegetables and water, a lot of seasoning is required. If you are familiar with different herbs and seasonings, don't be afraid to experiment.

Great Bean Soup

2 lbs. navy beans, washed & sorted
1 ham bone (with meat on) or 1 meaty ham hock
1 Tbs. Minors ham base (or other brand)
1/2 cup grated carrot
Salt to taste, if needed
1 onion, chopped
1/2 cup celery, diced
1/2 tsp. pepper

Use 6- or 8-quart stock pot or dutch oven. Pour washed beans into pot and cover with water. Soak overnight or at least 4 hours. Drain and put back in pot. Cover with 4 quarts fresh water. Add remaining ingredients; cook on med. to med.-low for 2 to 3 hours or until beans are tender. Mash beans with potato masher to make a heavier broth. Add water as needed during cooking as well as more seasoning, including ham base or salt. Add bacon bits for more flavoring. Serve with hearty bread and fruit salad.

Chicken Soup with Noodles

6 chicken thighs with the skin
1 pkg. noodles, cooked
4 quarts water
1 Tbs. Minors chicken base
    or 2 bouillon cubes

1 onion, diced small
1/2 cup grated carrot
1/2 cup celery, diced small
1/2 tsp. pepper
Salt as needed

Place everything in stock pot or dutch oven and bring to boil. Reduce heat to med. low and cook about 3 hours. Add desired size noodles.

Great Quick Chili

2 lbs. ground round
1 lg. onion, chopped
1 green pepper, chopped
1 Tbs. veg. oil
Salt and pepper
1 tsp. chili powder

1 can Brooks Chili Mix, 30 1/2 oz.
2 cans Brooks Chili Beans, hot
    or mild, 30 1/2 oz.
1 can Brooks diced tomatoes,
    just for chili, 14.5 oz.
1 or 2 cans water, to thin as desired

In 6-quart dutch oven, lightly saute onion and green pepper in oil to give a transparent look, one or two min. Add ground round. Break apart in pan using wooden spoon and leave in chunks as you move it around. Add salt, pepper, and chili powder, sprinkling on meat as you turn it. Cook until all pink is gone on med. high heat. Remove fat from pan with a baster. Add all can goods and 1 can of water. Mix well on high heat until it begins to bubble and mix well. Using second can of water, thin to desired consistency. Add about 1 more teaspoon chili powder. Simmer 1/2 hour to 1 hour. Ready to serve. Makes about 5 qts. or 15 to 20 servings. Freeze in quart containers for future meals. Keeps well 2 or 3 days refrigerated.

Easy Coleslaw

1 med. head cabbage, shredded
1 small onion, diced finely
1 carrot, finely shredded

1/4 tsp. dill weed or dill juice
1/2 to 1 cup Marzetti slaw
    dressing (as desired)

Mix all ingredients and stir well.

Easy New England Clam Chowder

1 can cream of potato soup
1 can cream of celery soup
1 can New England clam chowder
1 small can evaporated milk
1 small can whole kernel corn

1 can minced clams, pureed
   half of water in can
1 Tbs. butter
Optional: 1/2 cup each of celery
   and broccoli, steamed
   and cut in pieces

Mix all ingredients in pot and heat well. Serves 4 to 6. Because of the salt in canned soups, you shouldn't have to add more, although onion salt or celery salt works well. Sprinkle pepper on top and stir through.

Waldorf Salad

1/2 head iceberg lettuce, shredded
3 stalks celery, chopped
2 large Washington Delicious apples,
   chopped
1 cup cucumber, chopped

1 cup walnuts, chopped
1/2 cup raisins (optional)
1/2 cup seedless grapes
1/2 to 1 cup Marzetti slaw
   dressing (as desired)

Toss all ingredients together. Beautiful served in a crystal bowl and side dishes, as part of a meal, or on crystal plates, as an entree. Nice with hard crust rolls.

Black Bean Soup
Compliments of Lower Town Grill

2 cups black beans
8 cups water
1 Tbs. chicken base
1 onion, chopped
2 stalks celery, chopped

2 carrots, chopped
1 large bag frozen corn
2 Tbs. olive oil
2 tsp. salt
1/2 tsp. pepper

Seasonings: chili powder, cumin, thyme, parsley, bay leaf

Place beans, water, onion, salt, pepper, and chicken base in stock pot or dutch oven. Bring to boil, reduce heat, and simmer for 2 hours. Add water as needed. In skillet, saute carrots and celery in olive oil. Stir in seasonings. Add to soup pot. Bake frozen corn on cookie sheet until golden brown and add to soup. Simmer another hour until beans are easily crushed.

Deviled Eggs

6 eggs, hard boiled and chopped   **1 tsp. horseradish sauce**
1/4 cup onion, chopped fine   **1 Tbs. Miracle Whip**
Salt and pepper, sprinkled lightly   **(more if desired)**

Boil eggs (well covered with water) for 10 minutes with a metal spoon in pan to keep them from cracking. After 10 minutes, drain and let set 5 minutes in pan. In sink, run cold water over eggs, crack and peel under running water. Place on paper towel and allow to dry and cool. Cut eggs in half lengthwise and dump yolks into small mixing bowl. Place whites on egg platter or plate. Chop yolks and add all other ingredients. Mix well with fork. Drop mixture by spoonfuls into egg white shells. Shape as desired. Sprinkle top with paprika and chill. For variation, add a little dill pickle juice (1/2 tsp.), bacon bits or green pepper, finely chopped.

The Art of Making Gravy
Harry Reginald Searles

To prepare thickening mixture:
1 Tbs. cornstarch = 2 Tbs. flour

For example, to thicken 1 quart of liquid, use 1/2 cup of cornstarch stirred into 1/2 cup of cold water or 1/2 cup of flour stirred into 1 cup cold water, shaken. Cornstarch mixes instantly with water and can be stirred. Flour and water should be shaken in gravy shaker or covered container to eliminate lumps. Pour water in container first.

To prepare meat or chicken, season meat or chicken and let sit at room temperature for about an hour. Use a dutch oven to cook meat when making gravy. Heat 2 Tbs. oil on high. Add meat and brown on both sides. Cover while browning as it will brown nicely. Cook meat to recipe instructions at reduced heat. During the last 10 or 15 minutes, turn heat to high and brown meat again to get a nice base of drippings for the gravy. Remove meat to covered dish to keep warm while making gravy, mashed potatoes, and serving the vegetables. Reserve juice from potatoes and vegetables in separate pan to use in making gravy.

With heat still on high in dutch oven, brown the drippings and add 1 Tbs. Kitchen Bouquet to drippings. Add reserved juices to hot pan. Stir with wooden spoon to loosen drippings. Add 1 cup of cold water to juices to cool enough so that when you add thickening, it won't lump. Immediately when you add cold water, begin stirring the thickening into the juices. When you reach desired thickness, sprinkle salt and pepper on top and stir in. If a darker gravy is desired, add a little more Kitchen Bouquet. Boil 5 minutes. Gravy is ready to serve.

Entrees, Casseroles, Meats, & Vegetables

Rapid Grinding and Pulverizing Mills

No. 1, - $2.25
Capacity of Hopper
4 oz. Coffee

Highly Ornamented and Handsome in Appearance.

No. 2, $3.75
Capacity of Iron
Hopper,
4 oz. Coffer

Enterprise Mills are strong, do their work evenly, and can be regulated to grind course or fine, or pulverize, by means of a screw.

No. 2 1/2 - $5.00
Capacity of Nickel-
plated Hopper,
7 oz. Coffee

These Mills will grind 6 oz. Coffee per minute.

Grinders Warranted Equal to Steel.

Fried Potatoes and Onions

8 med. potatoes, peeled and dried on paper towel
1 med. onion, chopped or sliced

Cut potatoes like french fries, only half as long. Cook in hot oil about 1/4 inch deep in electric fry pan or heavy large skillet until golden crisp, turning over every few min. Add onions last 10 min. of cooking time and stir. Total cooking time is about 30 to 40 min. on med. high. Note: Place cover "turned" to allow some steam to escape. Covering tightly causes potatoes to be soggy. Serves 6 to 8. Good anytime, with anything.

Baked Potato

Wash with vegetable brush and puncture with fork so potato will not explode. Rub with vegetable oil for crisp skin. Bake at 400° preheated oven for approx. 1 hour, depending on size.

Mashed Potatoes

Place 6 or 8 potatoes in covered pot and cover with water. Add 1 Tbs. salt. Bring to boil and cook about 30 to 40 minutes, reducing heat to med. or med. high. Drain and save water if making gravy. Use potato masher or mixer, add a little milk and butter to taste, and whip well.

Creamed Potatoes

Cut potatoes in chunks. Cover with water and add salt. Cook covered until tender, about 30 min. Drain and put into casserole. Cover with white sauce and sprinkle parsley over the top.

Potato Patties

Use leftover mashed potatoes. Add 1 egg, chopped onion, and bacon bits. Fry in heavy skillet with cooking oil about 1/4 inch deep, medium to medium high heat. You can be creative and try kernel corn or other vegetables chopped in. Fry them crisp.

Boiled Dinner

Resembles a hearty soup. Serve with a hearty bread or homemade biscuits.

2 beef shanks, with round bone and marrow
1 large onion, sliced lengthwise
6 or 8 carrots, sliced
4 stalks celery, sliced
1 small rutabaga, cut in squares
2 cups fresh green beans, cut
1 cup cabbage, shredded
1 or 2 large cans stewed tomatoes, to taste for 1 or 2 pots
1 or 2 Tbs. Minor's beef base or 8-10 bouillon cubes
Salt and pepper to taste

Season and brown beef shanks in small amount of oil in 6-quart dutch oven. Cover with water and sliced onion. Let simmer for about 1 hour. Have a teakettle of water handy for adding as needed. After 1 hour, add carrots, rutabaga, and celery and fill pot with water to within a couple of inches from the top. Add beef base, salt, and pepper to taste. Simmer for another hour, add rest of cut up vegetables, stewed tomatoes, additional water, beef base, salt and pepper as needed for lots of broth and flavor. Continue to simmer another hour or so until all vegetables are tender and the broth is plentiful and rich with flavor. Total cooking time is 3 to 4 hours. Note: Because of all the vegetables and because you'll want a lot of broth, the pot may runneth over! If it does, split between 2 pots. Serve with love and candlelight. Wonderful for several days. Be sure to freeze some in containers for future meals.

Stove Top Pot Roast Dinner

3 or 4 lb. English cut or chuck roast of beef
Salt and pepper
1 large onion, sliced
8 carrots, cut in half
8 medium potatoes
1 Tbs. beef base or 2 bouillon cubes
1 tsp. kitchen bouquet (optional, for color and flavor)

Preheat a little oil in 6-quart dutch oven. Season meat with salt and pepper. Brown meat on both sides with cover on pan for about 10 or 15 minutes each side. Add enough water to just cover roast. Add sliced onions and reduce heat to medium-low; simmer 1 hour. Turn meat over and cook another hour. Add water as needed during cooking. Add carrots, potatoes, bouillon, kitchen bouquet, and cover all vegetables with additional water as needed. Cook another hour or until everything is tender with a fork. Baste with baster often during the last hour of cooking. When all is cooked, remove roast to large platter and cover with foil. Increase heat to medium-high and brown carrots and potatoes. Add vegetables to platter with meat or put in a covered casserole to keep warm and moist. Return heat to high to brown drippings. Use baster to remove excess fat. Add water or juice from any vegetables you may have cooked, or if you decided on mashed potatoes, drain potato juice into pot to help thicken gravy. Use cornstarch and water or flour and water, mixed, to thicken and make gravy. Season with salt and pepper stirred in and add a little kitchen bouquet as desired. Note: To serve as a leftover, cut meat into gravy, (thin with a little water), and add carrots and cut up potatoes. Simmer about 15 minutes. Serve as a hot beef sandwich over sliced bread or with mashed potatoes. Can be frozen for later use.

Meatball Stew
Barb Searles

2 lbs. ground beef or round steak
1 small onion, chopped fine to go into meatballs
1 medium onion sliced to cook with potatoes
Lawry's Seasoned salt or salt and pepper
1 egg
6 or 8 potatoes, cut in 1/8 chunks
1 tsp. salt added to potato water
    Boil potatoes in a 4 or 5-quart pan or dutch oven, well covered with water (about 1 inch above potatoes) to allow room for meatballs to be added. Add sliced onions and salt. Cook covered about 20 minutes or until almost done. While potatoes are cooking, prepare seasoned flour in deep mixing bowl and set aside. This is your meatball coating. In another mixing bowl, combine ground beef, finely chopped onion, seasoned salt, pepper, and egg. Mix well and form into walnut size meatballs. Drop meatballs into flour mixture and coat well. Immediately drop coated meatballs into potato pot and cook another 15 or 20 minutes, until potatoes and meatballs are cooked through. Reduce heat to medium. Thickened with either flour or cornstarch and water. Great with fresh cooked or canned green beans or broccoli flowerets, added to the pot or served on the side. A good hot, complete meal. This dish is not spicy and contains no butter or oil.

Pan Broiled Steak

Prime tenderloin, porterhouse or sirloin, 3/4 inch to 1 inch thick
    To tenderize well, sprinkle meat lightly on both sides with soy sauce or another meat tenderizer and work into meat with rounded bottom of a

spoon. Season lightly with garlic powder, seasoned salt or regular salt and pepper. Butter both sides and let sit about 15 min. Preheat a heavy skillet or grilling pan with grooves. Cook on medium high heat: approx. 3 min. each side for rare, approx. 5 min. each side for medium rare, approx. 6 min. each side for medium, and 8 to 10 min. each side for well done. When in doubt, cut with steak knife to check for doneness. Different cuts of meat can vary the cooking time. To serve, pour the drippings over the meat. This method is the most flavorful, but is not a low-fat method.

Chicken Chow Mein
Marilyn Sackett

4 chicken breasts, boneless and skinless, cubed
1/2 cup celery, chopped
1 can chow mein vegetables
1 can water chestnuts
1 cup fresh bean sprouts or 1 can bamboo shoots
1/4 cup cornstarch with 1 Tbs. water
1 tsp. soy sauce
Chow mein crisp noodles, canned or packaged
2 Tbs. butter or vegetable oil
In wok or electric fry pan, saute cubed chicken in butter or oil. Season lightly with garlic powder, salt, and pepper. Add all other chopped and canned ingredients. Stir with wood spatula. Mix cornstarch, water, and soy sauce in measuring pitcher and stir into all ingredients. Simmer 10 to 15 min. Serve with crisp noodles on top so they stay crisp. Note: If you wish to serve with rice, it becomes chicken chop suey!

Twice Baked Potatoes

4 med. potatoes, scrubbed clean and oiled
1/2 pint sour cream + 1 Tbs. melted butter
4 strips bacon, cooked crisp and crumbled
1 Tbs. chopped chives or green onions, mixed into sour cream
1 small onion, chopped or more green onion
Salt and pepper to taste (a little garlic salt is good)
2 Tbs. grated cheddar cheese or parmesan cheese
Bake potatoes at 400° for 1 hour. Skin should be crisp. When baked, cut in half and scoop out into mixing bowl. Place empty shells on cookie sheet and set aside. Add bacon, onion, salt, and pepper. Toss with a fork and mash or use a mixer. Add sour cream mixture with chives and finish mixing. Fill potato shells using a spoon. Top with grated cheese. Sprinkle a little paprika on top. Bake another 30 min. at 350°.

Creamy Au Gratin Potatoes

Sauce:
2 Tbs. cornstarch
2 cups milk
4 Tbs. butter
1 cup Velveeta cheese, cut up and packed
1/2 cup shredded, medium sharp cheddar cheese
Salt and pepper, sprinkled on top and stirred in
　　　　Put cornstarch in 2-quart saucepan and add milk. Stir over med.-high heat with a wooden spoon or spatula until blended. Add butter and sprinkle salt and pepper on top. Add Velveeta cheese, stirring constantly. Cook until thickened and pour over potatoes and onions.

Potatoes:
Peel and dice 6 or 8 potatoes into large pieces and put into adequate size casserole. Add 1 small onion, sliced or diced. Season potatoes and onions with Lawry's Seasoned Salt and pepper sprinkled lightly throughout. Add shredded cheddar cheese. Add cheese sauce to potato mixture. Bake at 350° for 1 hour or until potatoes are tender. Serve with a green vegetable or tossed salad. Nice with breaded pork chops and applesauce.

Chili Mac
Phyllis Searles

1 lb. ground round
1 large onion, chopped
1 can, 4 oz. mushroom pieces, drained
1 can, 16 oz. tomatoes, chopped
1 can, 8 oz. tomato sauce
1 or 2 Tbs. chili powder (optional)
1 can, 12 oz. red kidney beans, drained
Salt and pepper
2 cups elbow macaroni, cooked separately and drained
　　　　Cook macaroni in large pot of boiling, salted water. In dutch oven, lightly saute onion in hot oil. Add ground round. Season and brown. Add rest of ingredients and simmer for about 20 min. Add cooked macaroni to sauce. Serve with a tossed salad and hearty bread.

Low Fat Fettucini Alfredo

16 oz. pkg. fettuccini noodles
1 stick butter or margarine
1 cup 2% milk
Garlic salt and garlic powder, to taste
3/4 cup parmesan cheese
Pepper, add as desired

Cook noodles in 6 quarts of boiling water, with 2 tsp. salt, per package instructions. Add 1 Tbs. oil to water to keep noodles from sticking together. Stir often. Drain and return to pan. On low heat, add remaining ingredients. Note: Stirring in the butter and milk and adding the cheese over low heat helps to thicken. If a thinner consistency is desired, add a little more milk. Serves 6 or 8. Can be refrigerated and warmed up as desired for several days.

Fettucini Alfredo
Betty Castle

3/4 lb. fettucini noodles   **6 Tbs. unsalted butter**
2/3 cup whipping cream   **1/2 tsp. salt**
1 Tbs. garlic powder, or to taste
1/2 tsp. pepper   **1/4 tsp. nutmeg**
1 cup fresh parmesan cheese, grated   1 Tbs. fresh parsley, chopped

Cook noodles in 4 quarts boiling water, with 1 tsp. salt and 1 Tbs. oil., for 6 to 8 minutes. Drain and return to pot. In heavy saucepan, mix, butter, cream, salt, pepper, nutmeg, and garlic powder. Blend over medium heat, stirring constantly until it bubbles, for about 2 minutes. Stir in parmesan cheese. Pour over fettuccini and mix over low heat until mixed. Serve with salad or, for variation, stir in broccoli flowerets or spinach with fettuccini. Serves 4.

Stretch Burgers
Phyllis Searles

1 lb. ground beef   **1 med. onion, chopped fine**
1 egg   **1/2 cup milk**
1 Tbs. flour, rounded (use more if needed)
Salt, pepper, garlic powder, sprinkled lightly

Mix all ingredients in a bowl. Use an ice cream scoop and drop into frying pan with med.-hot oil. Flatten with spatula. Cook through on both sides for about 8 to 10 min. Good with chili sauce or horseradish. Nice with sliced tomatoes and coleslaw or salad.

The Plymouth Heritage Cookbook

During the depression years of the early 1930's, families were larger. Many, many people were out of work for long periods. The everyday concern was stretching the food supply as far as it could go. Thus, came the "stretch burgers" and "salmon patties," which could double the number of people you could feed with a smaller amount of meat. However, they were so tasty that they became family favorites.

Salmon Patties
Phyllis Searles

1 can Alaskan Sockeye Red Salmon   1 egg
1 onion, chopped fine   6 Premium soda crackers
       Mix together in bowl. Use ice cream scoop to place in frying pan with med.-hot vegetable oil. Season lightly with salt and pepper. Cook lightly on both sides. Serve with tartar sauce or a white sauce (see pages 10 and 11) and a tossed salad. Patties can be floured before cooking.

Meat and Vegetable Pie or Pasties
Mabel Ammon

Crust for 1 nine inch pie or 4 small pasties:
2 cups flour   1/2 cup shortening
1/2 tsp. salt   6 Tbs. cold water
       In large bowl, blend all ingredients with pastry blender. Shape two crusts using a rolling pin for top and bottom of pie. Cut in rounds for pasties. Spoon cooked meat and vegetables into rounds, fold over, and pinch edges together to seal.

Filling:
4 potatoes, diced
1 cup rutabaga, diced
1 small onion, sliced
1 lb. cooked ground beef, seasoned with salt and pepper
Butter for flavor on vegetables (1 pat for each pasty)
       Boil vegetables together and brown meat separately. Cook vegetables in lightly salted water and season again when assembling into pie crust. Add butter at this time. Bake 30 min. at 375° or until golden brown.

Swiss Steak
Barb Searles

1 or 2 lbs. round steak (can be cubed)
3/4 cups flour, seasoned with salt and pepper
1 large onion, sliced
1/4 to 1/2 cup vegetable oil
Cut meat into serving sizes. Season with garlic salt and pepper. Coat with seasoned flour. Heat oil in electric frypan and brown floured meat on both sides. Add sliced onion, cover with water, and reduce heat to simmer for 2 hours or until meat is tender. Add mushrooms, if desired. This dinner makes its own gravy. Serve with boiled or mashed potatoes.

Quick Baked Beans

2 lg. cans Bushe Pork and Beans with bacon and onions
1 med. onion, chopped
1/2 cup brown sugar (dark preferred)
1 tsp. prepared mustard
1/2 cup catsup
2 Tbs. bacon bits
1 Tbs. molasses (optional)
3 or 4 hot dogs, cut in 1 inch pieces
Mix all ingredients in 4-quart casserole. Bake at 325° for 1 hour, covered. Uncover and reduce heat to 300° for 1 hour. These beans can also be cooked in crockpot, one hour on high and 2 to 3 hours on low. Also good with 1 lb. of ground round, seasoned and cooked in skillet, then added to beans instead of hot dogs.

Green Beans and Bacon

1 lb. green beans, washed and cut
6 strips of bacon
Cook bacon crisp, drain, and set aside. Pour off some of the bacon drippings into cup to discard. Cover green beans with water in a 2-quart saucepan and cook, covered, until tender. Drain green beans and pour into skillet with bacon. Toss until beans are flavored and serve. Do not over-cook beans. They are better if they are a little crunchy.

Chop Suey
Marilyn Sackett

1 or 2 lb. package stewing beef   1 large onion, sliced
2 lbs. fresh bean sprouts or 3 cans, drained   2 stalks celery
Beef bouillon or base to taste
Season with salt, pepper, and soy sauce

In a 6-quart dutch oven, brown meat in oil and soy sauce, lightly seasoned with salt & pepper. Cover with water and simmer about 1 hour with onion and bouillon added. Add diced celery and water as needed. Simmer another 15 min. Add bean sprouts and simmer till tender, about 10 min. Thicken with cornstarch, water, and soy sauce mixed in cup. Start with about 1 Tbs. cornstarch and 1/2 cup water. This may be thick enough. Serve over steamed white rice or with chow mein noodles. Hot mixture can be served over fresh pea pods and rice. Pea pods become soggy if cooked in hot mixture.

Fried Cabbage and Kielbasa

1/4 lb. bacon, cut in 1 inch pieces
1 onion, sliced
1 small to medium head cabbage
1 pkg. of 2 Echrich beef kielbasa, cut in 2 inch chunks

In electric fry pan, cook bacon until crisp. Remove and drain on paper towel. Set aside. Cook cabbage, onion, and kielbasa until cabbage is tender at about 300°, stirring occasionally. Return bacon to pan, lower heat, and simmer for about 30 min. If you wish to reduce the fat content of this meal, pour most of bacon fat out of pan before adding other ingredients and parboil kielbasa and remove skin, slice into 2 inch chunks and add.

Meatloaf Dinner

2 lbs. ground round   1 Tbs. horseradish sauce
1 lg. onion, chopped   1 Tbs. catsup
1 green pepper, chopped   2 cans Campbell's Golden
2 eggs   Mushroom soup
10 Premium saltine crackers,   Salt and pepper
     crushed   6 med. potatoes, cut in half
1/2 cup bread crumbs   6 carrots, cut in half
1 Tbs. mustard

In large mixing bowl, break up the ground round. Season lightly with salt and pepper. Add all the chopped vegetables, crackers, seasonings, and 1/2 can of the soup. Mix well and shape into a firm loaf. Add potatoes and carrots around the loaf and the rest of the soup with enough water to cover the vegetables. Bake in an oval roasting pan at 350°, basting occasionally for 1 and 1/2 hours, uncovered. Reduce heat to 325° and cook another 1/2 hour. Vegetables should be oven browned. Remove to large platter using a large spatula. Put potatoes and carrots in covered serving bowl to keep warm. To make gravy, brown remaining drippings and add 2 cups of water and 1 Tbs. Kitchen Bouquet for flavor and color. Use wooden spoon to loosen drippings and thicken with either flour or cornstarch and water. (Flour mixture: 1/4 cup flour to 1 cup water. Cornstarch mixture: 2 Tbs. to 1 cup water.) Serves 6 to 8 people

Creamed Tuna on Toast

1 can tuna, 12 oz. white Albacore in water
1 pkg. frozen peas
French or Italian white bread, toasted
Sauce:

2 Tbs. butter or margarine	**2 cups 1/2% low fat milk**
4 Tbs. flour	**Salt and pepper**

Melt butter and add flour, stirring quickly with wooden spoon. Add milk gradually, stirring constantly. Continue to cook until sauce begins to thicken a little. Add tuna, cooked peas, and sprinkle salt and pepper lightly to cover top of sauce. Simmer and stir on low heat about 7 more minutes. Serve on toasted wedges arranged on plate. Serves 4 to 6. Leftover sauce should be used in a couple of days.

Skillet Candied Yams
Richard Sackett

4 large yams	**1/4 cup water**
1 cup dark brown sugar	**1/2 tsp. salt**
1/2 stick butter	

Bake potatoes about 40 min. Remove skins and set aside. Mix remaining ingredients in heavy skillet or electric fry pan until syrup boils. Add yams, quartered. Turn often until they are carmel-coated, approx. 20 min. Serve in covered casserole. Can be prepared ahead and warmed in microwave just before serving. Serves 6 or 8.

Macaroni and Cheese
Donna Perry

2 cups uncooked macaroni (makes 4 cups)
2 quarts water
1 tsp. salt
1 Tbs. oil

In 4 to 6 quart pan, bring water to rapid boil. Add salt, oil, and macaroni. Oil keeps noodles from sticking together. Cook 6 to 8 min., stirring often. Drain and rinse with cold water. Pour into spray-greased casserole or baking dish. Set aside. Preheat oven to 375°.

Cheese sauce:
2 Tbs. butter or margarine
2 Tbs. flour
2 1/2 cups milk (low fat works fine)
1 cup Velveeta cheese, shredded or cut in small pieces
1 cup shredded sharp cheddar cheese
Salt & pepper, 1/2 tsp. each

In 2-quart saucepan, melt butter. Stir in flour with wooden spoon. This will thicken very quickly, so have milk ready and pour a little at a time, stirring constantly. When mixture begins to bubble and thicken, add salt, pepper, and cheese. Pour cheese sauce into macaroni and mix well. Sprinkle a little parmesan cheese or some of the cheddar on top. Bake at 375° for 20 to 30 min. until nicely browned on top. Serve with green vegetables or a tossed salad. Makes 6 to 8 servings.

Country Steak

2 lbs. round steak, cubed
1/2 cup flour, lightly seasoned with salt and pepper
Garlic powder

Season cubed round steak with salt, pepper, and garlic powder. Cut steak into serving size pieces and coat with seasoned flour. Pour vegetable oil about 1/4 inch deep into heavy skillet or electric frypan. On high heat, place meat in hot oil and brown on each side. Reduce heat to med. and cook until tender with fork, about 10 or 15 minutes. If you use a lid, set it ajar to let steam escape. Remove from pan to platter and cover with foil to keep warm or place in casserole with cover. Note: Use a sharp knife or cubing mallet to cube steak or have the butcher cube it for you. This is a chewy, flavorful steak and will be a family favorite.

To serve with mashed potatoes and gravy, turn heat on high again to brown drippings. Add a little Kitchen Bouquet to drippings and stir with wooden spoon. Drain potato water into pan and any other vegetable juice from vegetables being served with dinner. Broccoli or cauliflower juice gives great flavor to your gravy. You can add water to make more. Thicken with flour or cornstarch and water. Sprinkle salt and pepper on top and stir in while cooking. Stir constantly while boiling and don't worry about little chunks of meat in the gravy as it enhances the flavor. Gravy can be made darker by adding a little more kitchen bouquet or lighter, like a milk gravy, by adding milk.

Roast Pork

Select pork loin or pork butt. Use dutch oven, electric roaster or other roasting pan. Season meat with salt, pepper, and garlic powder. Dust with flour and season again. Preheat 2 Tbs. oil in roasting pan and brown meat well on all sides. Brown meat covered between turning it. Cook at 350° for 20 minutes per pound, basting every 20 minutes. Add water as needed. Reduce heat to 325° and continue cooking and basting for another hour until tender. To serve, slice and arrange on platter with sliced apple rings or applesauce. Drippings make a wonderful gravy!

Stuffed Cabbage

1 large head cabbage   **1 tsp. baking soda**

Bring 2 quarts water to boil in 4-quart pan with baking soda added. (The baking soda in the water neutralizes the gas in the cabbage.) Immerse whole cabbage in boiling water for about 15 min. or until leaves are softened and can be pulled off easily. Peel off about 10 or 12 leaves. Set aside.

2 lbs. ground chuck or round	**10 Saltine crackers, crushed**
1 onion, chopped fine	**1 envelope Lipton Beefy Onion soup**
1 green pepper, chopped	**3/4 cups water**
1/2 cup uncooked rice	**Lawry's Seasoned Salt and pepper**
2 eggs	**1/2 cup bread crumbs sprinkled through meat**

Mix the onion soup in water. In large bowl, mix all ingredients. Use ice cream scoop or spoon and put onto cabbage leaves. Roll closed, tucking in the ends and fasten closed with toothpicks. Place in dutch oven and cover with the following:

1 can, 15 oz. tomato soup   **1 can, 15 oz. V-8 juice**

Simmer 2 1/2 to 3 hours. Makes 6 servings of 2 each. Serve with hearty bread or hard crust rolls and fruit or Waldorf salad.

Pork Chop and Scalloped Potato Casserole

6 med. potatoes, cut in small chunks
2 Tbs. butter
1 1/2 to 2 cups milk
1 large onion, sliced
4 Tbs. flour
Salt & pepper, sprinkled on
each layer
4 pork chops - 3/4 inch thick, season garlic powder, salt and pepper

In casserole or baking dish, layer half of potatoes and onion, and sprinkle flour with spoon. Dot with pieces of butter, sprinkle with salt and pepper, and add half of the milk to cover. Repeat for second layer. Place seasoned pork chops on top. Bake at 400° for 1 hour or until pork chops are browned. Turn pork chops and brown on the other side, 1/2 hour or so. Test potatoes with fork for doneness. Serve in casserole with a green vegetable and applesauce or spiced apple rings. Serves 4.

Kraut and Kielbasa (or Sausage)
Vivian Pringle

1 pkg. Echrich kielbasa or sausage,
cut up
1/4 lb. bacon
1 med. onion, chopped
1 large can diced tomatoes
with juice
1 pkg. sauerkraut, lightly
rinsed and drained
1 med. green pepper, chopped
(optional)
Garlic powder, salt, and
pepper to taste

Cook kielbasa and bacon together in dutch oven until bacon is crisp. Drain off the fat. Add remaining ingredients to the pot with meat. Cook all in one pot. Reduce heat and simmer for approx. 1 hour. Wonderful at picnics!

Braised Short Ribs

3 lbs. beef short ribs
1 tsp. salt
1/2 tsp. pepper
1 tsp. garlic powder
1 cup flour
2 med. onions, sliced
4 carrots, halved
4 potatoes, quartered
1 cup water

Put flour, seasonings, and short ribs in bag and shake. Brown the coated ribs in fry pan with a little oil. Put potatoes, carrots, and onions in crockpot first, then the short ribs. Add water, cover, and cook on low, 7 to 10 hours. On high, cook 4 to 6 hours. Remove everything to a casserole and make gravy. Serve with gravy poured lightly all over.

Lennie Bowser

Swiss Steak with Tomatoes

2 lbs. round steak, cubed
   and fat trimmed
1 cup flour
Salt & pepper

1 can, 15 oz. stewed tomatoes,
   Italian style
1 jar Heinz Brown Gravy
1/2 cup water

Cut meat into serving size pieces. Season with salt and pepper. Mix flour, salt, and pepper in deep mixing bowl and toss with fork. Coat meat with flour mixture and pound with cubing mallet or sharp knife. Brown meat in electric fry pan on both sides. Add 1/2 cup water and simmer about 10 min. Put stewed tomatoes, gravy, and 1/2 can water in blender. Blend for about 30 seconds. Place meat in baking dish or pan and cover with the tomato and gravy mixture. Bake at 325° for about 3 hours.

Rice Pilaf

1 whole chicken
2 or 3 chicken bouillon cubes
1 stick butter

1 pkg. tiny noodles
1 cup rice, uncooked

In stock pot or dutch oven, cover chicken with water and add bouillon cubes. Bring to boil and cook with cover for about 2 hours or until tender. Remove chicken and de-bone. When chicken is cooled, place in container and put in refrigerator. Cool the broth, skim the fat from top, and put in refrigerator until the next day. In skillet, melt butter, add 1 pkg. tiny noodles, and brown. Add broth, chicken, and rice. Simmer 1 hour, covered.

Hungarian Goulash
Vivian Pringle

2 lbs. ground beef
1 medium onion, diced
2 cans red kidney beans

3 cans tomato soup
3 cans water

Brown meat with onions. Season with salt and pepper. Add rest of ingredients and simmer for about an hour. Serve with dumplings (cooked on top), noodles or mashed potatoes.

Grilled Pork Loin Bistro Style
Compliments of Greg & Susan Goodman, Owners of Cafe Bon Homme

5 lbs. pork tenderloin
1/4 cup ground dry mustard
1/8 cup curry

1/8 cup cumin
1 tsp. crushed black pepper
3 oz. honey

Rub pork tenderloin with honey. Mix dry ingredients thoroughly and rub onto pork. Refrigerate for six hours. Grill or sear pork until brown. Finish in 400 degree oven until medium doneness. Serves 6 to 8.

Atlantic Swordfish with Pepper Infusion
Compliments of Greg & Susan Goodman, Owners of Cafe Bon Homme

4–6 oz. center cut swordfish steaks
1 red pepper
1 yellow pepper
1 green pepper
1 red onion, small

1 cup kalamata olives
1 1/2 cup artichoke hearts
2 oz. white wine
1 oz. olive oil
Crushed black peppercorns

Julienne cut all peppers and red onion thinly. Slice olives in half, lengthwise. Crush whole black peppercorns. Rub swordfish with olive oil. Push crushed pepper evenly into both sides of swordfish. Grill or pan-sear swordfish over high heat. Saute peppers, artichoke hearts, onion, and olives. (Deglaze pan with white wine.) Place vegetable mixture on plate. Remove swordfish from grill or pan and set on top of vegetables. Finish with fresh lemon juice if desired. Serves 4.

15 Minute Patio Chicken Dinner
Florence Yaconis, Westland, MI

3 whole chicken breasts, split, boneless & skinless
4 Tbs. butter
1 Tbs. minced onion
1 green pepper, cut in strips
1 cup celery, sliced diagonally
1 cup chicken broth (use 1 or 2 bouillon cubes to 1 cup water)
4 1/2 oz. can pineapple chunks, syrup included
2 Tbs. cornstarch + 2 Tbs. water, set aside in measuring cup
1 Tbs. Worchester sauce, added to cornstarch and water
4 oz. can pimento, chopped
1 tsp. Accent

Cut chicken in strips and season with garlic powder, salt, and pepper. Heat butter in electric fry pan and sautee seasoned chicken strips until white on high heat. Add onion, green pepper, and celery. Stir until tender, about 2 to 3 minutes. Add Accent, chicken broth, and pineapple with syrup. Bring to boil, cover, and cook 5 minutes on medium-high. Add cornstarch mixture and stir rapidly. Cook another 5 minutes. Add pimento pieces for garnish. Serve over cooked rice, noodles or mashed potatoes. Serves 6.

Easy Meatloaf

2 lbs. ground round   1 large onion, chopped
1 green pepper, chopped   2 eggs
10 Premium saltine crackers, crushed
1 can Hunt's Ready Meatloaf Fixin's
1/2 tsp. garlic powder, sprinkled on meat
Salt and pepper, sprinkled to taste
1 cup water and 1 envelope onion soup mix

Mix all ingredients in large bowl. Use clean hands and work through well. Place in dutch oven and shape into loaf. Add 1 cup water or onion soup around loaf. Add more water if needed. Add only enough water to keep meat from burning. Bake at 350° for 1 hour. Baste occassionally. Reduce heat to 325° and cook another 30 minutes, basting a couple of times. Remove to platter and slice to serve. Drain fat out of pan, leaving drippings and loose bits of meat. Add 1 Tbs. Kitchen Bouquet and brown drippings well for gravy. Great with mashed potatoes and a vegetable or two. Use juices from potatoes and vegetables plus 1 cup of water to make gravy. Note: If you use a loaf pan to cook in, do not add water or liquid as there is obviously no room. There will not be gravy drippings.

Baked Ham

1 whole or half ham, Wet Virginia brand, semi-boneless, pre-cooked
1/2 cup brown sugar   6 or 8 whole cloves
1 can sliced pineapple,   1/2 cup Vernor's gingerale
     with juice reserved

Score the ham using a sharp knife and slice on an angle through outer layer on the fattiest side, one inch apart, all the way across. Repeat slicing at opposite angle. Place ham in deep roasting pan and rub with brown sugar. Push whole cloves into knife grooves to form a staggered design. Add reserved pineapple juice and gingerale to pan, pouring over the ham. Add water as needed to maintain juice in pan. Cook ham at 325° for 2 1/2 hours, basting every 20 minutes. Cook at 350° for another 30 minutes. Remove ham to cutting board and let sit 15 minutes. Slice and place on platter with pineapple rings. For ham gravy, brown drippings well, add Kitchen Bouquet, vegetable juices, and 2 cups water. Thicken, season with salt and pepper, and boil for 5 to 10 minutes.

Cheese Ravioli
Compliments of Ernesto's Italian Country Inn

Olive oil	**Eggs**
Garlic	**Ricotta cheese**
Onions, chopped fine	**Marscipone cheese**
Leeks, chopped fine	**Ricotta Pecorina cheese**
Spinach, washed and chopped	**Parmesan cheese**
Salt and pepper	**Pasta dough**
	Sage Sauce

Saute onions, leeks, and garlic slowly, carmelizing them. Add spinach and sautee. Let cool. Add cheeses and eggs and mix thoroughly. Stuff pasta. After cooked, serve with Sage Sauce. (Sautee heavy cream and butter and let reduce. Add fresh or dried sage and a touch of nutmeg.)

Smoked Salmon-Parsnip Rounds
Compliments of Ernesto's Italian Country Inn

3 parnsips (about 3/4 lb.)	**1/4 tsp. pepper**
1/4 tart apple	**2 Tbs. butter**
1/4 small onion	**1/4 cup vegetable oil**
1/3 cup flour	**1/4 lb. smoked salmon**
2 eggs	**Chives or dill sprigs for 1 tsp.**
Salt	**garnish**
3/4 cup creme fraiche or sour cream	

Peel and coarsely grate parsnips in bowl. Grate in apple and onion. Toss and sprinkle with flour. Lightly beat the eggs and add. Add salt and pepper and toss to combine well. In a large fry pan, heat butter and oil. Make pancakes using about 1/2 tsp. batter for each. Flatten with the back of a spoon to make irregularly shaped 2 inch rounds. Cook until golden brown, 2 to 3 minutes per side. Cook remaining rounds, adding more butter and oil to pan if necessary. They can be made ahead. To reheat, put them on baking sheets and heat in preheated 400° oven until crisp. To serve, cut salmon into one inch by 1/4 inch strips. Chop chives or dill. Top each cake with 1 tsp. creme fraiche or sour cream. Lay 2 strips of smoked salmon in a cross over the creme and sprinkle with chives or dill.

Cappelini Pomodoro 'e' Basilico
Compliments of Ernesto's Italian Country Inn

Toss cappelini pasta with Ernie's Marinara Sauce (see page 39), add fresh basil, and serve.

Peasant Pasta
Compliments of Ernesto's Italian Country Inn

Olive oil	**Red crushed pepper**
Garlic	**Black pepper**
Parsley	**Salt**
Dried basil	**Canned plum tomatoes, with**
Dried oregano	**a little juice**
Fresh basil	**Ladle of Marinara sauce**
Dried thyme	

Saute garlic in oil, then crush dry ingredients and put in pan. Add tomatoes and sauce. Simmer 3 to 5 minutes. Add pasta, toss, and serve.

Easy Barbecued Spareribs

3 - 4 lbs. spareribs, cut in serving sizes
Garlic salt and pepper
1 onion, sliced
1 bottle of barbecue sauce (16 oz.)
1/2 cup brown sugar

Lightly season ribs and place in broiler pan lined with foil. Add a little water to pan, with rack placed at about center of oven. Broil ribs for about 30 min. to remove some of the fat and to brown. Place browned ribs in a crockpot. Add onion, barbecue sauce, and brown sugar. Stir to mix well. Cover and cook on low for 6 to 8 hours or on high for 3 to 4 hours. Serve with a tossed salad or coleslaw and spiced apple rings. Also good with a baked potato, a green vegetable, and applesauce. Serves 4.

Advice from turn-of-the-century Woman's Club Cook Book.
KNOX ACIDULATED GELATINE saves the cost, time and bother of squeezing lemons

Eggplant Sandwiches
Compliments of Ernesto's Italian Country Inn

Flour seasoned with salt and pepper
Eggs, beaten
Bread crumbs (see recipe below)
Eggplant
Fresh basil, chopped
Garlic, minced
Anchovies, minced
Fontina cheese, sliced 1/8 in. think
Marinara sauce (see recipe below)

Peel and cut eggplant into coins of 3/8 inch thickness. While heating your skillet, dredge eggplant through flour, then the eggs, then back into the flour. Repeat this process with all eggplant rounds. Place oil in the heated skillet and fry eggplant until they are 3/4 cooked. Remove from skillet and place on paper towel to drain excess oil. Next, spread a mixture of basil, garlic, and anchovies onto 1/2 of the eggplants, place a piece of cheese over this spread, and then place the other piece of eggplant on top to form a sandwich. Dip each sandwich in the eggs and bread crumbs. Fry these again until both sides are golden brown. Place some marinara sauce on a plate with the sandwiches with a dab of sauce of each.

Bread crumbs:
Dry bread crumbs
Parmesan cheese
Salt and pepper
Flat leaf Italian parsley
Fresh chopped onion

Marinara Sauce:
Olive oil
Canned Italian plum tomatoes packed in puree, crushed
Salt and pepper
Parsley
Fresh basil

Place oil in sauce pan and brown. Add tomatoes, salt, pepper, parsley, and basil. Simmer for 45 minutes.

Signature Veal Dish
Compliments of the Costanza Family of Station 885

6 oz. top round of veal, pounded until thin
1 Tbs. black olives, diced thin
1 Tbs. green olives, diced thin
1/2 tsp. garlic, diced
2 oz. white cooking wine
3 jumbo gulf shrimp
10 oz. veal stock (use beef stock if unavailable)
1 Tbs. butter

    In large, hot saute pan, add 1 oz. clarified butter. Add veal and shrimp and cook until tender. Add olives, garlic, wine, and stock. Reduce heat to medium-high and simmer 2 minutes. Remove from heat and stir in butter until melted.

Liver, Onions, and Bacon

1 or 1 1/2 lbs. baby beef liver, sliced
6 or 8 slices bacon
2 large Spanish onions, diced
1/4 stick butter or margarine
1/2 cup flour
Salt and pepper

    In large pan, melt butter, add onions, and saute to desired doneness. In a separate pan, cook bacon until crisp and drain on paper towel. Coat liver with flour and season with salt and pepper on each side. Cook liver in bacon drippings on medium-high heat. Brown on each side, then reduce heat and simmer 10 minutes. Place liver in first pan on top of onions. Place bacon on top of liver and cover. Simmer on low heat 15 to 20 minutes. Serve with steamed green vegetables or salad.

Speedy Spinach Lasagne
Compliments of Ronald G. Loiselle, Mayor of Plymouth

1 1/2 jars prepared spaghetti sauce
2 eggs
15 oz. Ricotta cheese or 16 oz. cottage cheese
1 bag fresh spinach, washed, stems removed, torn in small pieces
1/2 cup Parmesan cheese, grated
1 lb. Mozzarella cheese, grated
1 lb. uncooked lasagne noodles

In large bowl, mix chopped spinach, eggs, Ricotta or cottage cheese, and half of the Parmesan cheese. Cook noodles per package instructions. Place cooked noodles in bottom of baking dish and spoon sauce over noodles to cover. Spoon spinach mixture over noodles and sprinkle Mozzarella over all. Repeat layers ending with Mozzarella on top. Cover dish with lightly greased aluminum foil and bake at 350° for one hour or until noodles are tender. Let stand 10 minutes before cutting in squares. Serves eight.

Eggs,
Poultry,
&
Seafood

R. Beaubien
Wholesale and retail
ICE

Woodbridge West, foot Campau St., Detroit
I have a very convenient dock for loading and unloading vessels.
Also convenient for mooring boats during the winter season.

Polk, 1881 — Ice was harvested from an unpolluted Detroit
River in the last century.

Cooking Eggs

Soft Boiled

Place eggs in water and bring to boil. Cook 3 minutes for soft, liquid yolk or 5 minutes for firmer yolk.

Hard Boiled

Place eggs in water, bring to boil, and cook for 10 min. Drain and let sit for about 5 min. Run cold water over eggs to cool. Peel under cold tap water. Place on paper towel to dry. Cool before chopping.

Poached

Boil water, then crack shell and carefully drop in water. Reduce heat and baste or coddle eggs by spooning water over eggs until done, as desired.

Scrambled

Crack eggs into bowl, add 1 ice cube, and whip with wire whisk or fork. Remove ice cube and pour into fairly hot, preheated skillet with a little butter or oil. Use spatula to turn eggs over and push around until desired doneness is achieved. Great cooked in a little bacon fat when you are serving bacon.

Basic Omelette

1 onion, sliced or diced
1/4 cup green pepper, diced
Bacon, cooked crisp in separate pan, cut in pieces
1/4 to 1/2 cup shredded cheddar cheese (or your favorite)

Whip 5 or 6 eggs; set aside. Use an omelette pan that has two sides and closes. Put a teaspoon of butter in each side of omelette pan and saute vegetables. Pour equal amounts of the eggs into each side of pan and distribute the rest of the ingredients equally on both sides of pan. Put heat at med.-high to med. When eggs begin to set up a little, flip pan closed and cook on both sides with heat reduced to med.-low. Cook 3 to 5 min. or until lightly browned and cooked through. Cut into to check for desired doneness. Note: Leftover omelette can be refrigerated in a plastic bag or other container overnight and eaten next day. Warm in microwave. Good with chili sauce and toast. Also good with a little spinach or broccoli flowerets cooked in. Can be served for breakfast, lunch or dinner. Makes a good sandwich .

Chicken Parmesan Patties

4 cubed fresh chicken patties
1/4 cup Hellman's mayonnaise
Garlic salt and pepper, lightly sprinkled on patties
1/2 cup bread crumbs
2 Tbs. parmesan cheese, added to bread crumbs

In bag, place bread crumbs, cheese, and seasoning. Shake and set aside. Brush patties with mayonnaise and put into bag to coat. To bake, place patties in uncovered pan or dish. Bake at 400° for 15 to 20 minutes until golden brown. Turn only once during cooking. To grill, use about 2 Tbs. hot oil in fry pan. Cook about 3 minutes each side until golden crisp. Serve with salad or other side vegetables. Great as a sandwich on a toasted bun with lettuce and condiments as desired, and a pickle or tomato slice.

Chicken Noodle Dinner

4 chicken breasts, with skin and bones
1 carrot, chopped in small pieces
1 stalk celery, chopped
1 tsp. chopped garlic
1 tsp. garlic powder
1/2 tsp. garlic salt
1/4 tsp. pepper
1 Tbs. chicken base or 3 bouillon cubes
1 lg. pkg. wide noodles

Place chicken in 6-quart dutch oven or stock pot and cover with water 3/4 full. Add onion, carrots, celery, and all seasonings. Cover pot and bring to full boil, then reduce heat to med.-low. Cook 2 or 3 hours until chicken is very tender and falling from bones. Remove chicken from pot with slotted spoon into a large bowl and use 2 forks to break apart and remove all bones and skin. Turn heat to high. Add more water if necessary to 1/2 full. Taste broth at this time and add more seasoning, if necessary. Add noodles to boiling broth and return de-boned chicken to pot. Cook another 15 min., stirring occasionally until noodles are cooked. Makes 8 or 10 servings. Can be stored frozen in portions for other meals. Best served in shallow soup bowls on a dinner plate because of broth. Good with hearty bread and salad.

Chicken Paprikas

1 onion, chopped	1 tsp. salt
4 Tbs. shortening or oil	8 chicken thighs or breasts
1 Tbs. paprika	1 1/2 cups water
1/2 tsp. black pepper	1/2 pint sour cream

In dutch oven, saute onions in shortening, add seasonings and chicken. Saute chicken about 10 minutes, add water, cover and simmer until chicken is tender, about 20 minutes. Remove chicken, add sour cream to pan of drippings, and stir in well. Add dumplings to this mixture. Arrange chicken on top and cook another 10 minutes. Serves 4 to 6.

Dumplings

3 beaten eggs	1 tsp. salt
3 cups flour	1/2 cup water

Mix all ingredients well using large spoon. Drop by spoonful into about 1 quart of boiling, salted water. Cook about 10 minutes. Drain and rinse in cold water. Add to above recipe.

Easy Barbecued Chicken

4 chicken breasts, with or without bone, with fat trimmed
1 cup barbecue sauce
Garlic powder, salt, pepper

Season chicken with seasonings and place in crockpot. Cover with barbecue sauce. Cover and cook on low for 8 hours. For added flavor, remove to foil-lined broiler pan and broil 5 or 10 minutes. Serve with salad and rice.

Southern Fried Chicken and Milk Gravy

2 lbs. chicken, cut up   **2 Tbs. flour**
Flour, salt, pepper   **1 cup milk**
Vegetable oil 1/4 inch deep in fry pan   **1 cup boiling water**

Use deep electric or iron skillet for cooking. Use paper bag for flour, salt, and pepper to coat chicken. The secret to good, browned, fried chicken, is to flour twice. Put flour and seasoning into paper bag. Shake to mix. Add chicken and shake well. Remove chicken to dry, about 10 minutes, then replace in bag and shake again. Brown chicken, all sides, in hot oil. Reduce heat when nicely browned and cook uncovered for about 30 minutes. Turn occasionally. Remove chicken to platter and cover to keep warm. Pour off excess fat. For gravy, add 2 Tbs. flour and slowly add milk while stirring. When thickened, stir in water. If too thick, add more milk. Lightly sprinkle salt and pepper into gravy and stir in. Serve with mashed potatoes or biscuits.

Italian Chicken Bake

3 lb. package of chicken, cut up with skin removed
1 stick butter, melted
1 tsp. garlic powder, added to melted butter
1 cup Italian flavored bread crumbs
1/2 cup grated parmesan cheese
1 Tbs. parsley flakes

Sprinkle chicken with garlic salt and pepper and set aside. Stir garlic powder into melted butter. Mix bread crumbs, cheese, and parsley flakes. Brush each piece of chicken with garlic butter mix. Coat buttered chicken in bread crumb mixture. Bake in shallow dish or pan at 350° for 45 to 60 minutes. Turn once. Cook to golden brown and tender. Serves 4 to 6.

Broiled Chicken
Lori Nader

4 chicken breasts, with bone
1/4 cup butter, melted
Garlic salt and pepper to taste

Brush chicken breasts with melted butter. Season with garlic salt and pepper. Place on cookie sheet or in shallow pan on a sheet of foil. Bake at 350° for about 30 minutes. Test with fork for tenderness. Can be broiled with or without skin and without bone. Serves 4.

Honey Lemon Chicken
Compliments of Plymouth Landing

2 6 – 8 oz. fresh chicken breasts, boneless
1/4 lb. linguini   **Red pepper**
4 Tbs. butter   **Onion**
Green pepper   **Mushrooms**
Honey Lemon Sauce:
1/2 cup honey   **1/4 cup lemon juice**
1 cup water   **1 Tbs. cornstarch**
1 Tbs. chicken base   **1 pinch parsley**

Slice vegetables thinly and saute in melted butter to desired texture. Add salt and fresh ground pepper. Set aside. Boil linguini to desired doneness and drain. Grill chicken and cut into strips. Mix sauce ingredients in pot and bring to boil. Let simmer for 5 to 10 minutes. Add chicken strips to sauteed vegetables and stir. Add Honey Lemon Sauce and toss. Place cooked linguini on plate. On top of noodles, place vegetable and chicken mixture. Serves 2.

Salmon Loaf
Mabel Ammon

1 pkg. noodles, cooked and drained   **1 Tbs. minced onion**
2 lb. canned red salmon   **1 tsp. lemon juice**
4 eggs   **2 tsp. chopped parsley**
1 cup milk   **14 oz. cheddar cheese, shredded**
2 slices bread, crumbled

In mixing bowl, flake salmon with fork and add 2 beaten eggs. Add milk, bread, onion, lemon juice, and parsley. Salt lightly and mix well. Shape into loaf or pack into loaf pan. Add 2 beaten eggs to noodles and fold in cheese. Pour over salmon loaf. Bake at 375° for 1 hour. Serves 6 to 8.

Broiled Fish

Use salmon, halibut, cod, orange roughy or whitefish. Brush with melted butter, sprinkle with salt and pepper, and place in a well oiled, shallow pan or on a cookie sheet. Place in a preheated broiler oven 3 or 4 inches from heat. Broil until tender with fork, turning once or twice. Allow 8 to 10 minutes for fish steaks about 1 inch thick, 15 to 20 minutes for whole split fish. Note: If fish seems dry, brush a little more butter. Serve garnished with a little paprika on top and lemon wedges or with tartar sauce.

Poached Fish

Use whole fish, fillets or fish steaks. Grease a deep fry pan or electric fry pan. Season fish with salt, pepper, lemon juice, and other flavorings you might enjoy on fish. Place fish in fry pan and cover with equal parts of heated milk and water or equal parts of water and dry white wine. Simmer in covered pan about 5 to 10 minutes per pound or until tender.

Baked Fish

Brush fish with melted butter, season as desired, and coat with bread crumbs or your favorite coating. Place in shallow, well oiled pan. Bake 15 minutes for fish about 1 inch thick at 375°; 12 minutes for thinner fish; 25 minutes for thicker fish. Brush with butter if they dry out. Note: Always test with fork for doneness.

Pan Fried Smelt
Phyllis Searles

3 or 4 dozen fresh smelt   1/4 cup butter
3/4 cups flour   2 eggs
1 tsp. salt   2 Tbs. milk
1/2 tsp. pepper

Clean fish and slit open with scissors to remove backbone. Remove tail with scissors. In small bowl, mix eggs and milk. In large bowl, mix flour, salt, and pepper. In heavy skillet, heat butter to fry fish. Dip smelt into egg mixture, then into flour mixture, and place in skillet. Saute over medium heat for 2 or 3 minutes on each side or until golden brown. Do not cook too many at a time and, if needed, add a little more butter or vegetable oil to pan. Turn only once. Serve with a little paprika sprinkled on top and tartar sauce. Garnish plate with lemon wedges. Serves 4.

Pan Fried Perch
Phyllis Searles

2 or 3 lbs. lake or ocean perch   1/4 cup butter
3/4 cups flour   2 eggs
1 tsp. salt   2 Tbs. milk
1/2 tsp. pepper

Buy perch cleaned, fresh or frozen. Prepare and fry as above. Serves 4.

Jim's Whitefish
Compliments of Jim Plakas, Owner of Plymouth Landing

4 fillets fresh Michigan whitefish
Seasoned flour, with lemon pepper or your choice
2 Tbs. butter   **1/2 Tbs. lemon juice**
White wine   **Capers**
Salt and fresh ground pepper

Lightly dredge whitefish in seasoned flour. Melt butter in saute pan. Place fish in pan and add salt and pepper. Add capers, white wine, and lemon juice. Allow alcohol from wine to burn off leaving only the wine's fruit taste. Allow fish to cook until golden brown. Serve with steamed vegetables or rice pilaf, garnished with lemon wedges. Serves 2.

Breads,
Pies,
&
Pastries

The money and worry saved and the increased cleanliness of Gas over all other fuels ought to be sufficient to induce any thinking woman to

COOK WITH GAS

1907 advertisement

Pie Crust

2 cups flour
1/2 tsp. salt
1/2 tsp. baking powder

3/4 cups shortening or butter, cold
1/3 cup ice water

Use metal or glass mixing bowl. Mix flour, salt, baking powder, and shortening in food processor or with a pastry blender until mixture is flaky and looks like little beads. Add cold water and continue blending until dough barely sticks together. With clean hands lightly floured, shape into roll. Cut in half to make two crusts. Shape each into a flat, pancake shape. Roll out on lightly floured surface with floured rolling pin to about 1/8 inch thickness and to 1 inch larger than pie tin when pan is placed on rolled dough (upside down). While dough is rolled out, use fork to make air-vent holes. Fold dough in half, place in pie tin, and open up. Trim edge with knife. Makes two 8 or 9 inch pie shells.

For pie crust shells, pinch or flute edge with your fingers, dampened with water. Bake in hot oven 400° to 450° for 12 or 15 minutes. Fill shells with desired filling. Can be topped with meringue or whipped cream. Fruit filling can also be topped with strips of leftover pie dough and placed back in oven for additional baking per instructions of filling recipe.

For two crust pie, place top pie crust over filling and over bottom crust. Seal and flute edge. Bake per pie instructions. Dough can also be rolled out between two sheets of waxed paper. It is important to handle dough as little as possible as too much handling will toughen the crust. Prepare cold – bake hot! Pie crust and biscuit dough are certainly something you must acquire a "feel" for.

Sour Cream Doughnuts

2 eggs
1 1/4 cups sugar
2 Tbs. shortening or 1/4 cup veg. oil
3/4 cup sour cream
3 1/2 cups flour
2 Tbs. orange juice or 1 Tbs. grated orange peel

2 tsp. baking powder
1 tsp. baking soda
1/2 tsp. salt
1/2 tsp. nutmeg
1/2 tsp. cinnamon

In one quart measuring pitcher, mix all dry ingredients. In large mixing bowl, combine eggs, sugar, shortening, and orange juice. Add dry ingredients alternately with sour cream or to egg mixture. Beat just until blended after each addition. Roll dough out on lightly floured surface to 1/3 inch thickness using floured doughnut cutter or glass. Deep fry in hot vegetable oil, 375° for 1 1/2 to 2 minutes each side. Only turn once while cooking. Drain on paper towels. Serve plain, frosted or coated with powdered sugar.

Buttermilk Doughnuts

4 cups flour	**1/4 cups vegetable oil**
4 tsp. baking powder	**1 tsp. vanilla**
3/4 tsp. salt	**1 tsp. nutmeg**
1/2 tsp. baking soda	**1/2 tsp. cinnamon**
2 eggs, beaten	**1 tsp. grated orange rind**
1 cup sugar	

Follow above recipe. When doughnuts are cut, allow to stand about 5 minutes before cooking. A light crust forms and cuts down a little on fat absorption. Cook a few at a time. If oil is too hot, they will not cook through. If not hot enough, they will be fat soaked

Sour Cream and Yogurt Doughnuts

4 cups flour	**1 1/2 cups sugar**
1 tsp. baking powder	**1 1/2 cups sour cream**
1 tsp. baking soda	**1/4 cup vanilla yogurt**
1/2 tsp. salt	**2 eggs**
1/2 tsp. nutmeg	**1/4 cup vegetable oil**
1/2 tsp. cinnamon	

Place first six ingredients in food processor and pulse three times, five seconds each. Add sugar and pulse again for five seconds. Add rest of ingredients and repeat. Scrape sides of bowl as necessary with rubber scraper. Do not over process. Remove dough onto well floured board. If dough is too sticky to work with, work the flour into the dough, kneading and flattening. Roll dough out with floured rolling pin to 1/3 inch thickness. Cut with well floured doughnut cutter (flour cutter each time). Place cut doughnuts on a cookie sheet and let sit for about 30 minutes. Cook 3 or 4 doughnuts at a time and a few of the holes. If they are cooking too dark, reduce heat. Cook at 375° using a thermometer, for about one minute or so each side, and place on paper towel to cool and absorb as much of the oil as possible. These doughnuts are wonderful. Serve them plain or coat them with powdered sugar or cinnamon and granulated sugar. Shake in a plastic bag to coat. Or top with a dark chocolate frosting. Hint: If you coat with powdered sugar, do it twice. Makes 18 doughnuts and holes.

Banana Nut Bread

1 stick butter	3 ripe bananas, mashed
1 cup sugar	2 cups flour
2 eggs	1 tsp. baking soda
1 tsp. vanilla	1/2 tsp. salt
1/4 cup milk	1 cup chopped walnuts (more if desired)

Mix butter, sugar, eggs, vanilla, milk, and mashed bananas. Add flour, baking soda, and salt. Add walnuts when everything is well mixed. Bake in greased loaf pan at 350° for 1 hour. Test with toothpick. Note: For date and nut bread, replace bananas with 10 oz. pkg. Sunsweet pitted dates, chopped.

Banana Nut Cake

1/2 cup shortening	1/2 tsp. salt
1 1/2 cups sugar	1 cup bananas, mashed
2 eggs, well beaten	3/4 cup buttermilk
2 cups sifted flour	1 tsp. vanilla
1 tsp. baking soda	1/2 to 1 cup chopped walnuts

Mix all ingredients in bowl with electric mixer. Bake in two 8-inch layer cake pans, greased and lightly floured. Bake at 350° for 30 min. Test with toothpick. Frost with a butter or buttercream icing.

Date and Nut Bread

1 1/2 cups hot water	1/4 tsp. salt
1 tsp. baking soda	2 Tbs. butter
1 lb. dates, pitted and chopped	1 tsp. vanilla
1 1/2 cups sugar	3 1/2 cups flour
2 eggs, beaten	1 or 2 cups walnuts, as desired, chopped

Generously grease and flour 2 loaf pans and set aside. Boil water, add soda, and pour over chopped dates in mixing bowl. Let cool. Add sugar, eggs, salt, butter, and vanilla. Beat well. Add flour by spoonfuls to mixture. Fold in the nuts and pour into prepared pans, equally. Bake at 300° for 1 hour. Test with toothpick. Should be dry. Can be wrapped in foil and stored in refrigerator. Keeps about 1 week. Makes 2 loaves.

Date and Nut Loaf

1 1/2 cups chopped walnuts
1 cup dates, pitted and chopped
1 1/2 tsp. baking soda
1/2 tsp. salt
1/4 cup shortening

3/4 cups boiling water
2 eggs, beaten
1/2 tsp. vanilla
1 cup sugar
1 1/2 cups flour

Combine dates, nuts, soda, and salt in large mixing bowl. Add shortening and boiling water. Let stand 15 min. Stir to blend. Add vanilla to beaten eggs and pour into bowl. Mix sugar and flour together and add to bowl. Bake in loaf pan 1 hour at 350°.

Onion Corn Bread

1 large, sweet Spanish onion, sliced
1 pkg. corn muffin mix
1 egg
1/3 cup milk
1 cup cream style corn, canned
2 drops hot pepper sauce (optional)
1 cup sour cream
1/4 tsp. dill weed
1 cup sharp cheddar cheese, grated

Saute onion in 1/4 cup butter and set aside. Combine muffin mix, egg, milk, cream corn, and hot pepper sauce. Pour into pan. Add sour cream, salt, dill weed, and 1/2 cup of grated cheese to sauteed onions. Spread over batter and sprinkle remaining cheese over top. Bake in 8 inch square, greased pan at 425° for 25 to 30 minutes. Serve warm.

Cranberry Nut Bread

2 cups flour
1 cup sugar
1 1/2 tsp. baking powder
1/2 tsp. baking soda
1 tsp. salt

3/4 cup orange juice
2 Tbs. shortening
1 egg, beaten
1 1/2 cups fresh cranberries, chopped
1 cup walnuts, chopped

Mix flour, sugar, baking powder, baking soda, and salt in large mixing bowl. Stir in orange juice, shortening, and egg. Add cranberries and nuts. Bake at 350° for 1 hour, in greased loaf pan. Test for doneness with toothpick. Should be dry. Cool and remove from pan. Can be stored in refrigerator, wrapped in foil.

Casserole Bread

1 pkg. yeast	1 Tbs. butter
1/4 cup warm water	2 tsp. dill seed
1 cup cottage cheese, large curd	1 tsp. salt
2 Tbs. sugar	1/4 tsp. baking soda
1 Tbs. instant minced onion or fresh	1 egg
	2 1/2 cups flour

Use well greased 2-quart casserole. Soften yeast in water. Warm cottage cheese to lukewarm. In large mixing bowl, combine all ingredients except flour. Gradually add flour, beating well after each addition to form stiff dough. Let rise about 1 hour or until doubled in size. Stir down and turn into greased casserole. Let rise in warm place for 40 minutes. Bake at 350° for 40 to 50 minutes until golden brown. Remove from oven and brush with soft butter. Note: Grease hands lightly with oil to handle dough. Turn on oven light with no heat to make a good place to let dough rise.

French Toast

2 eggs	Dash of salt
1/2 cup milk	4 bread slices, cut diagonally

Mix eggs, milk, and salt. Dip bread wedges into egg mixture and place in hot oil. Reduce heat immediately to medium-high. Cook to golden brown and crisp on each side, turning a few times with fork. Serve with butter and powdered sugar or syrup. Also good with fruit syrup.

Scratch Pancakes

1 1/2 cups flour	1/2 Tbs. sugar
2 tsp. baking powder	1 egg
1/2 tsp. salt	1 cup milk
	2 Tbs. oil or melted butter

Mix all dry ingredients in 2-cup measuring pitcher. Add egg and mix. Add milk 1/2 at a time. Then add melted butter or oil; beat lightly with wire whisk. Use heavy med.-hot griddle. Pour small amount of oil on griddle or grill and spread with bunched up sheet of waxed paper. Set waxed paper aside and use each time you pour more batter. Pour batter to size desired. Flip over when bubbles appear. Take a peek at the underside to see if browned enough. When pancakes are flipped, the other side is done quicker. Serve immediately. Recipe can be doubled to serve more people. When making more, remove to plate or pan and cover with foil. Place on a warming tray or in a warm oven until ready to serve. Serve with warm syrup and butter, powdered sugar or a warm, fruity syrup. Apples or blueberries are very good added to the batter before cooking.

Quick Mix Pancakes

1 cup Aunt Jemima mix
1/2 cup Bisquick
1 egg

3/4 to 1 cup milk, as desired
1 Tbs. oil

Mix all ingredients and follow above directions.

Scratch Waffles

3 cups flour
5 tsp. baking powder
1/4 tsp. salt

2 eggs, separated
1 cup evaporated milk
1/2 stick butter, melted

Use quart size measuring pitcher. Whip egg yolks and milk. Whip egg whites stiff and fold into yolk mixture with melted butter. Bake in hot waffle iron until they quit steaming and top lifts easily, revealing golden brown waffles, about 3 to 5 min. To freeze, cook a little less and package in portions, 3 or 4 squares to a package. Use quart-size baggies. To reheat, put them in a toaster on med.-low to desired doneness. Serve with melted butter brushed on with pastry brush, warm syrup, powdered sugar or fresh fruit sauce. Makes 6 or 8 waffles.

Quick Mix Waffles

2 cups Bisquick or pancake mix
2 eggs
1 cup evaporated milk

1/2 cup water
1/2 stick butter, melted

In quart size measuring pitcher, mix all ingredients, adding melted butter last. Follow above directions for baking, serving, and freezing.

Diabetic Apple Pie
Barbara Mailhoux Drake

10 Empire apples, pared, cored, and chunked
1 Tbs. butter or margarine   1 pkg. Equal
1 tsp. cinnamon   1/2 tsp. nutmeg

Combine all ingredients in large bowl and mix well. Pour into prepared pie shells. Bake at 375° for 50 minutes or until crust is golden brown.

Cookies,
Cakes,
Candy,
&
Desserts

*Turn-of-the-century
hand-cranked
Cherry Stoner*

Lennie Bowser

Cream Puffs
Dot Ferraro

1/4 cup shortening   **2 eggs**
1/2 cup water   **1 tsp. salt**
1 cup flour

Place water, shortening, salt, and flour in 2-quart saucepan and boil together, stirring constantly until smooth. Beat in eggs, one at a time. Remove from heat. Drop by tablespoonful onto cookie sheet. Bake at 450° for 10 minutes, then at 400° for 25 minutes. When baked, fill with whipped cream, Cool Whip, custard or pudding.

Chocolate glaze topping: **2 Tbs. butter**
1 1/2 one oz. squares unsweetened   **1 1/2 cups powdered sugar**
   chocolate   **1 tsp. vanilla**

Use 1-quart pyrex pitcher. Melt chocolate and butter in microwave. Heat 2 minutes and stir. Repeat a couple of times so that mixture is hot and well mixed. Stir in powdered sugar and vanilla until crumbly. Blend in 3 tablespoons boiling water gradually to make a fairly heavy consistency. Pour quickly over top and sides of puffs.

Peanut Butter Pie
Lynn Johnson

4 oz. cream cheese   **1/2 cup milk**
1 cup powdered sugar   **8 or 9 oz. Cool Whip**
1/2 cup peanut butter

Blend cream cheese and sugar in mixer until smooth. Add peanut butter and milk and blend. Fold in Cool Whip. Pour into pre-baked graham cracker crust. Chill about an hour in refrigerator. Serve with chocolate syrup drizzled over top.

Mississippi Mud Pie
Char Briggs

Crust:
1 stick butter, melted   **1 cup pecans, chopped**
Layer #1:
11 oz. cream cheese   **1 cup powdered sugar**
1 tsp. vanilla   **1 cup Cool Whip**
Layer #2:
2 small pkg. instant chocolate pudding mix   3 cups milk

Mix crust ingredients and press into 10-inch pie tin. Bake at 350° for 20-35 min. until light golden brown. Mix layer #1 and spread on baked crust. Mix layer #2 and pour onto layer #1. Top with Cool Whip and shavings from a chocolate bar.

Mandarin Orange Cake

1 box yellow cake mix
1 can (11 oz.) Mandarin oranges with juice
4 eggs
1/2 cup vegetable oil

Mix cake mix, oranges with juice, eggs, and oil with mixer until orange slices are broken up and batter is fluffy, about 3 min. Bake in 9 x 14 in. cake pan sprayed with Bakers Pride or Bakers Joy spray. Bake at 350° for 20 to 30 min., until cake tests done with toothpick.

Topping:
1 can (20 oz.) crushed pineapple with juice
1 Cool Whip (8 or 9 oz. size)
1 pkg. instant vanilla pudding

Blend until well mixed. Place baked cake on a cookie sheet lined with foil and pour topping on cake just before serving.

Brownies
Debbie Sue Hershey

1 stick butter
1/3 cup cocoa
1 cup sugar
2 eggs
1/2 cup flour
1/2 tsp. salt
1/4 tsp. baking powder
1/4 tsp. baking soda

Use 8 inch square pan, greased. Melt butter and stir in cocoa. Set aside. Mix sugar and eggs in mixing bowl. Mix flour, salt, baking powder, and baking soda in a cup. In mixing bowl with sugar and eggs, add butter and cocoa, and flour mixture. Mix well and pour into pan. Bake at 350° for 20 to 25 min. Test with toothpick.

Baked Custard Pudding
Phyllis Searles

3 eggs, slightly beaten
1/2 cup sugar
1/4 tsp. salt
2 cups whole milk, scalded
1/2 tsp. vanilla
Nutmeg or cinnamon

Combine eggs, sugar, and salt. Add scalded milk and vanilla. Strain into 1-quart casserole. Sprinkle with nutmeg. Place casserole in pan of hot water. Bake at 325° for 40 minutes. Knife should come out clean. Serves 6.

Boiled Custard

1 quart whole milk	1 tsp. vanilla
3/4 cup sugar	Pinch of salt
3 eggs, well beaten	

Heat milk until hot. Add sugar to beaten eggs. Add enough warm milk to sugar and beaten eggs to heat mixture (prevents curdling). Pour into hot milk, stirring constantly, and cook to desired consistency. Pour through strainer and cool, adding vanilla and pinch of salt. Serve with whipped cream. Note: To triple recipe, add 2 extra eggs.

Baked Cheesecake

Graham Cracker Crust:

2 1/2 cups graham cracker crumbs	6 Tbs. sugar
2/3 cup butter, melted	

Mix in bowl with fork. Press into 9 x 14 inch baking dish or pan or use 2 nine inch pie tins. Butter the baking pans before pressing mixture in. Do not bake. Chill 1 hour before filling.

Filling:

24 oz. cream cheese	1 cup + 2 Tbs. sugar
5 eggs	1 Tbs. + 1 1/2 tsp. vanilla

Cream together and pour into baking pans. Bake at 350° for 30 min.

Topping:

1 pint sour cream   1 tsp. vanilla   6 Tbs. sugar

Mix together, spread on cooled cheesecake, and place in oven. Bake another 10 min. at 400°. Can be served with fresh strawberries (slightly blended) and pour over top. If you make 2 nine inch cheesecakes, you can freeze one by wrapping in double foil. Best used within a month.

Raspberry Cheese Pie
Patricia Stokes

16 oz. cream cheese	1 cup sugar
2 eggs	1 can raspberries, drained well
1/2 tsp. lemon peel	2 tsp. vanilla

Make graham cracker crust in pie dish. Whip cream cheese and add eggs, lemon peel, sugar, and vanilla. Mix until creamy. Gently add 1/2 can of raspberries to mixture. Pour into crust and bake at 375° for 35 to 45 minutes. Center will not be firmly set. Chill 3 to 5 hours. Top with whipped cream and remaining berries.

Rice Pudding
Compliments of The Plymouth Landing

1 quart milk	1/3 cup rice
1/3 cup sugar	1/2 tsp. salt
1 tsp. vanilla	1/2 cup cream or evaporated milk

Nutmeg or cinnamon to garnish

Slowly heat milk. Add rice, sugar, and salt. Cook over low heat for 45 minutes, stirring occasionally. Add vanilla and cream. Allow to cool and garnish.

Walnut Raisin Sweet Rolls
Compliments of Tina & Nick Ristich, Owners of the Cozy Cafe

1/2 cup butter	1 tsp. salt
1 cup milk	4 cups flour
3 eggs, beaten	1 pkg. yeast (1/4 oz.)
1/2 cup sugar	2 cups brown sugar

Cinnamon, raisins, walnut pieces, in desired amounts

In a cup, melt together butter and milk. In large bowl, mix eggs, sugar, and salt. Soften yeast in 1/4 cup warm water with 1 tsp. sugar and set aside to bubble. Add 2 cups flour and the milk/butter to egg mixture. Add yeast mixture also when yeast bubbles. Mix well. Add the remaining 2 cups flour and mix until soft, sticky dough is formed. Roll into circle and cut into 8 pie-shaped pieces. Sprinkle with cinnamon and brown sugar. Add raisins and walnuts. Roll each wedge starting at wide end. Allow to rise one hour or until doubled in size. Bake on cookie sheet at 350° for 15 to 20 minutes. Drizzle with powdered sugar glaze (1 cup powdered sugar with 1 to 2 Tbs. milk). Serve warm.

Sweet Butter Icing

1/2 cup milk	1/4 cup sugar
1 1/2 tsp. cornstarch	1 tsp. vanilla
1/2 lb. sweet butter, unsalted	

Stir milk and cornstarch constantly over med. heat. Allow to cool slightly. Cream rest of ingredients and beat with mixer into milk mixture until fluffy.

Buttercream Icing
Donna Perry

1 egg white	1 stick butter
1 cup sugar	1 stick Crisco
3/4 scalded milk	

Beat egg white until stiff and add sugar (do not mix). Add scalded milk (do not mix) and put in refrigerator to cool. Cream together butter and Crisco in separate bowl or measuring cup. Add mixtures together and beat at med. speed until thick. Will curdle before it thickens. Spread immediately. Note: To scald milk, bring to boil so that cream comes to top and then remove from heat.

Another Buttercream Icing

1/3 cup water	2 Tbs. butter
2 Tbs. cornstarch	1 1/2 cups sugar
1 cup scalded milk	1 1/2 cups shortening
1 tsp. vanilla, almond or coconut flavoring	

Mix water with cornstarch. Add scalded milk. Melt butter in pan and add scalded milk. Cook, stirring constantly until it becomes a cream sauce. Add sugar; stir until dissolved. Chill in refrigerator. In separate bowl, mix shortening and pour cold cream sauce over top. Add vanilla, almond or coconut flavoring and blend on high until to make a good spreading consistency. Makes enough for a 9 inch layer cake.

Chocolate Cake
Barb Searles

1/3 cup firm shortening or soft butter	Hot water
1 1/2 cups sugar	1 1/2 cups flour
2 eggs	1 tsp. baking powder
1 tsp. vanilla	1 tsp. baking soda
1/2 cup cocoa	1/2 tsp. salt
1 rounded tsp. instant coffee	1 cup milk, soured with 1 tsp. vinegar

In bowl, mix shortening or butter, sugar, eggs, and vanilla. In a small cup, mix cocoa, coffee, and water. In a separate bowl, mix flour, baking powder, baking soda, and salt. Add flour mixture alternately with sour milk to mixing bowl with shortening, sugar, eggs, and vanilla. Then add cocoa mixture. Bake in 9 x 13 inch cake pan or two 8 inch layer cake pans, well greased. Bake at 350° for 30 to 35 min. Test with toothpick.

1 – 2 – 3 – 4 Cake

1 cup shortening	2 tsp. baking powder
2 cups sugar	1/2 tsp. salt
3 cups flour	1 1/4 cup milk
4 eggs, separated	1 1/2 tsp. vanilla

Cream sugar and shortening well. Add egg yolks and beat again. Pour vanilla into milk and add to dry ingredients. Fold in beaten egg whites. Bake at 350° for 30 to 40 min. Test with toothpick. Makes two 9 inch layers plus 1/2 dozen cupcakes or a high 9 x 13 inch sheet cake. A good, old fashioned yellow cake.

Oatbran Cookies

1 cup butter, softened	3/4 cup All Bran, crushed
1 cup dark brown sugar	1 tsp. baking soda
1 cup granulated sugar	1 tsp. cinnamon
2 eggs	1/2 tsp. salt
1 tsp. vanilla	1 cup walnuts, chopped
2 cups flour	1 cup raisins (optional)
3 cups Quaker Oats	

Cream butter and both sugars. Add eggs and vanilla, mix well. Mix flour, baking soda, salt, and cinnamon, and add to mixture. Mix well. Add oats, bran, walnuts, and raisins gradually, mixing well with each addition. Scoop walnut size balls. Roll with palms and place on cookie sheet; flatten with fork. Bake in preheated 350° oven on bottom rack, 12 to 15 minutes. When baked, cool on cookie sheet a few minutes then remove to paper towel. Store in plastic container. Crunchy and yummy!

Bachelor Buttons
Inez Matthews

1/2 cup shortening	1 tsp. vanilla
1 cup brown sugar	1 tsp. creme of tartar
1 tsp. baking powder	2 1/4 cups flour
2 eggs	

Mix all ingredients together in food processor. Shape into roll, cover, and refrigerate about an hour. Scoop up with baller or teaspoon and make balls the size of a walnut or smaller. Place on cookie sheet. Use round end of a wooden spoon and press down in center. Fill with your favorite jelly. Bake at 350° for 10 to 12 minutes or until lightly browned.

Lennie Bowser

Old Fashioned Sugar Cookies
Char Briggs

3 cups flour	**1 cup butter**
1 cup sugar	**1 egg**
1 1/2 tsp. baking powder	**3 Tbs. milk**
1/2 tsp. salt	**1 tsp. vanilla**

In food processor or pastry blender, combine flour, sugar, baking powder, salt, and butter. Mix to dough consistency. Add egg, milk, and vanilla. Blend another few seconds. Form into a roll, cover, and refrigerate for about an hour or until you are ready to bake. Will keep for about a week. Roll out with a rolling pin (floured), to 1/8 inch thickness or less. Cut in shapes with cookie cutters and place on cookie sheet. Bake at 375° for 8 to 10 minutes or until brown around the edges. Makes 3 to 4 dozen.

Russian Tea Cakes
Char Briggs

1 cup butter
1/2 cup powdered sugar
1 cup powdered sugar, in separate bowl to roll in
2 1/4 cups flour
1/2 cups walnuts or pecans, chopped
1 tsp. vanilla

Mix butter and 1/2 cup powdered sugar. Add flour, salt, nuts, and vanilla. Mix well. Form into balls, walnut size, and roll in powdered sugar. Bake at 400° for 8 to 10 minutes. Remove as they are baked and roll again in powdered sugar. Place on waxed paper until set and cooled.

Hermits
Char Briggs

1 cup brown sugar	**1/2 cup raisins**
1/2 cup shortening or butter	**3 cups flour**
1/2 cup hot water	**1/4 tsp. salt**
1 tsp. baking soda	**1 tsp. cinnamon**
2 eggs, well beaten	**1 tsp. baking powder**

Cream butter and brown sugar. Add hot water, baking soda, eggs, and raisins. Add flour, salt, cinnamon, and baking powder. Drop by generous teaspoons or tablespoons for small or large cookies. Bake at 375° for 10 to 12 minutes on greased cookie sheet. Makes 34 to 48 cookies.

Chocolate Cookies
Char Briggs

1 egg
1/2 cup shortening
1/2 tsp. salt
1/2 cup sour milk

1 cup brown sugar
1 2/3 cups flour
1/2 tsp. baking soda

2 oz. unsweetened chocolate or 6 Tbs. cocoa + 2 Tbs. shortening

In small saucepan, mix shortening, chocolate, and vanilla. Melt and set aside. In large mixing bowl, beat eggs and sugar until light. Add chocolate mixture alternately with flour and salt. Drop by spoonfuls onto cookie sheet. Bake at 350° for 10 minutes. Makes 2 1/2 dozen.

Peanut Butter Cookies

1/2 cup butter
1/2 cup peanut butter, creamy
1/2 cup sugar
1/2 cup brown sugar
1 egg

1/2 tsp. vanilla
1/2 tsp. salt
1/2 tsp. baking soda
1 cup flour

Cream butter, peanut butter, and both sugars. Stir in egg, vanilla, salt, baking soda, and flour. Drop by spoonful and press flat, using a fork. Bake at 350° for 10 minutes in preheated oven. Makes 1 1/2 dozen.

Chocolate Peanut Butter Fudge

9 cups granulated sugar
2 1/2 sticks butter
3 small cans (5 oz.) evaporated milk
2 large bags Nestle chocolate chips
1 large bag butterscotch chips or other chocolate chips
1 large bag (22 oz.) mini marshmallows
1 large jar of peanut butter, melted in microwave
3 or 4 cups walnuts, chopped (not too fine)

In 6-quart dutch oven, mix sugar, butter, and milk. Bring to a rolling boil, stirring often. Reduce heat a little and cook another 5 to 7 min. During last 2 minutes, add rest of ingredients. Remove from heat when everything has been added. Tear off 6 sheets of foil, about 18 inches each, and line up ready to pour fudge onto. Mix well with large sturdy wooden spoon and pour onto foil. Let set and cool before cutting. Wrap each foil package and store in refrigerator. This recipe makes a great deal of fudge and can be stored in the refrigerator for a week or two.

Old Fashioned Cocoa Fudge

4 cups sugar
3/4 cup Hershey's cocoa
1 stick butter
2 cups evaporated milk or
    1 can = 12 oz. + 4 oz. regular milk
3/4 cup cold water for testing

1/4 tsp. salt
1 Tbs. vanilla

    In a deep, heavy saucepan, mix sugar, cocoa, and salt with a wooden spoon. Add milk. Bring to a rolling boil on high heat. Reduce heat to medium-high and continue cooking approximately 30 min., stirring often and scraping sides of pan. Add 1/2 of butter. Fudge will boil up near top of pan and will stir down. After 30 min., fudge will take on a different, thickened look. Let some drip into the cup of cold water to test. When it forms a soft ball, it is time to remove from heat.

    Add rest of butter and vanilla; stir in and let stand 5 min. or so. Now beat until nicely thickened and fudge begins to lose its shine, about 5 min. Pour and spread quickly onto cookie sheet greased with butter. Let set and cool about 15 min. and cut into squares. Note: Cooking and setting time for this type of fudge can vary. During the beating time, the fudge loses some of its shine. Pour quickly when this happens. You will get a feel for it with this recipe.

Cocoa Peanut Butter Fudge

4 1/2 cups sugar
1/3 cup Hershey's cocoa
1 cup evaporated milk
2 sticks butter
2 pkg. dark Nestle chocolate chips
1 cup mini marshmallows
2 cups peanut butter, melted in microwave
2 or 3 cups walnuts, chopped not too small
1 Tbs. vanilla

    Mix sugar, cocoa, butter, and milk. Bring to rolling boil, stirring often. Reduce heat and cook 7 minutes. During last 2 minutes, add marshmallows, chocolate chips, and peanut butter. Remove from heat and stir in vanilla and walnuts. Mix well. Pour immediately onto 3 large sheets of aluminum foil, equally. Form, wrap, and allow to cool before cutting. Store in refrigerator up to 2 weeks.

Chocolate Chiffon Cake
Linda Zancanaro

1 3/4 cups sifted flour
1 1/2 cups sugar
1 3/4 tsp. baking powder
1/4 tsp. baking soda
1/4 cup Crisco oil
4 sq. unsweetened chocolate, melted
1 cup walnuts or pecans, chopped finely

1 1/2 cups milk
2 cups eggs, separated
1 tsp. vanilla
1/2 cup sugar
1 tsp. salt

Sift flour, sugar, powder, soda, and salt in large mixing bowl. Add oil and 1 cup milk and beat one minute, scraping constantly. Add remaining milk, egg yolks, vanilla, and chocolate. Beat egg whites until frothy. Gradually add 1/2 cup sugar. Continue beating until stiff and glossy. Fold egg white mixture into flour mixture until thoroughly blended. Fold in nuts. Pour batter into baking pans (tube pan or 2 8-inch round cake pans), sprayed with Bakers Joy. Bake 35 to 40 minutes at 350°. Test with toothpick. Frost with butter cream icing or other favorite icing.

Whole Wheat Applesauce Muffins
Carolyn Loesch

1/2 cup oil
3/4 cups brown sugar
1 cup applesauce

1 1/2 cups whole wheat flour
1 tsp. baking soda
1 tsp. cinnamon

Mix oil and sugar; add applesauce and soda. Stir in flour and cinnamon. Preheat oven to 375°. Grease and flour muffin pan and fill half full. Bake for 20 minutes. Makes 12 muffins.

Beverages

Dandelion Wine

6 qt. of flowers
4 qts. of water
    let stand for 3 days and
       3 nights then strain and add
4 lbs sugar
2 sliced lemons
2 tablespoons of yeast
    let stand 4 days and
       4 nights then strain again.
Then bottle.

Elder Blosson Wine

1 qt. blossoms
1 gal water
1 lemon
    let stand 24 hours then strain
    then add yeast and sugar

Courtesy of Plymouth Historical Museum

Kahlua

1 1/2 cups brown sugar
1 cup sugar
2 cups water, boiled 5 min.

1/2 cup decaf instant coffee, cooled
2 Tbs. vanilla
3 cups vodka

Blend all ingredients in blender and pour into glass container. Wait for 24 hours before serving. Serve over ice or after dinner in a cup of black coffee, topped with whipped cream, and sprinkled with grated chocolate.

Carbonated Fruit Punch

1 quart pineapple juice
1 quart lemonade
1 cup orange juice
1 Tbs. lime juice
1 large club soda

1 large gingerale
13 oz. pkg. strawberry jello
1/2 cup sugar, to taste
1 cup fresh strawberries

Combine all ingredients in 8-quart stock pot. Add 1 cup ice cubes. Blend well with electric mixer. Pour into juice containers and store in refrigerator until ready to serve. Pour over ice in a punch bowl. Note: Strawberries can be left whole and floated in punch.

Bailey's Irish Creme

1 pint coffee cream
1 1/2 cups whiskey
1 can Eagle Brand milk

1 1/2 Tbs. chocolate syrup
3 eggs
1 tsp. vanilla

Blend whiskey, eggs, syrup, and vanilla in blender. Add cream and milk for 10 seconds. Serve chilled over ice, after dinner, with candlelight.

Another Bailey's Irish Creme
Vivian Pringle

1 can Eagle Brand Milk
1 tsp. chocolate syrup
1/2 tsp. coconut extract

5 eggs
1/2 pint whipping cream
1 cup whiskey

Blend milk, chocolate syrup, coconut, and eggs in blender. Add whipping cream and whiskey. Continue to blend another 30 seconds. Store in refrigerator up to 3 months. Serve chilled over ice.

Tom Collins
Dot Ferraro

1 shot (1 oz.) gin or vodka	1/2 tsp. lemon juice
1 tsp. powdered sugar	1/2 cup Collins mix or Seltzer
1/2 cup orange juice	water

Mix in blender and pour over ice in tall glass. Garnish with a slice of lime or lemon, a cherry, and a straw.

Bacardi Punch

1 1/4 cups light rum	1 1/2 cups crushed ice
2 cups orange juice, fresh or frozen	1 1/2 tsp. grenadine

Mix in blender or cocktail shaker. Serve in stemmed margarita glasses. Serves 6 to 8.

Wedding Champagne Punch

4 bottles champagne	2 bottles Canada Dry gingerale
2 bottles white wine	1 ice ring

Fill a jello ring mold with water and freeze. Chill ingredients. To serve, place ice ring in punch bowl, pour all ingredients over top, and stir. Makes 73 three oz. servings.

Egg Nog

8 eggs, separated	1 1/2 quarts milk
2 cups sugar	2 1/2 pints cream, whipped
1 1/2 cups rum or whiskey	Sprinkle of nutmeg (optional)

Beat egg yolks and sugar until light. Slowly add rum or whiskey (this cooks the yolks). Add milk, fold in whipped cream, then stiffly beaten egg whites. Chill. Stir thoroughly before serving because cream and egg whites will rise to top. Sprinkle with nutmeg.

Index

Wedding Champagne Punch, 70
White Cream Sauce, 10
Whole Wheat Applesauce Muffins, 67

About the Author

Evelyn "Lennie" Bowser began cooking while standing on a chair at her mother's stove when she was only six years old. At the age of twelve, she baked cakes from scratch, decorated them, and sold them to her neighbors.

She began her writing career as a member of the Young Writers Club, sponsored by *The Detroit News*, at the age of nine. Many of her stories and poems were published. In junior high, she worked on the school paper and also self-published a neighborhood paper before she was a teenager.

As a young girl, she worked as a waitress and moved to management, eventually owning and operating two restaurants. She worked in the restaurant business for 27 years. Now in retirement, Lennie has combined her love for cooking and writing with her love for her community.